D0853172

Cartels of the Mind

Cartels of the Mind

Japan's Intellectual Closed Shop

IVAN P. HALL

 W · W · Norton & Company · New York · London

For Mara and Ben

Copyright © 1998 by Ivan P. Hall

For information about permission to reproduce selections from this book,
write to Permissions, W. W. Norton & Company, Inc., 500 Fifth Avenue,
New York, NY 10110.

The text of this book is composed in Sabon with the display set in
Bernhard Bold Condensed and Optima
Composition by Tom Ernst
Manufacturing by The Haddon Craftsmen, Inc.

Library of Congress Cataloging-in-Publication Data

Hall, Ivan P., 1932–
Cartels of the mind: Japan's intellectual closed shop / Ivan P. Hall.
        p.   cm.
Includes bibliographical references and index.
ISBN 0-393-04537-4
1. Japan—Civilization—1945–   2. National characteristics, Japanese.
3. Japan—Relations—Foreign countries.   I. Title.
DS822.5.H338   1997
952—dc21   97-2436
                                                                          CIP

W. W. Norton & Company, Inc., 500 Fifth Avenue, New York, N.Y. 10110
http://www.wwnorton.com

W. W. Norton & Company Ltd., 10 Coptic Street, London WC1A 1PU

1 2 3 4 5 6 7 8 9 0

Contents

Introduction

"NORMAL COUNTRY"
Foreign Intellectuals Need Not Apply

As Washington and Tokyo sort out their new power relationship and respective roles in post–Cold War Asia, the time has come to turn a spotlight on those intellectual barriers, both institutional and more subtly psychological, that Japan continues to maintain against the entire outside world, Western and Asian alike. These "cartels of the mind"[1]—an entire parallel world of obstacles resembling and helping to sustain the better known market barriers—serve neither the professed new goals of Japan nor those of the United States.

Despite their repeated promises of "internationalization," Japanese legal, media, university, and research organizations continue to maintain an intellectual shop closed to genuine participation by foreign lawyers, journalists, professors, students, and scientific researchers. That Japanese intellectuals maintain these barriers with enthusiastic conviction, and with no visible desire to reciprocate the open access they themselves enjoy in other countries, simply confirms the depth of Japan's insular mentality. And when foreign observers pull the wraps off these and other embarrassing matters, Japanese cultural, media, and political leaders are more likely to pounce on the critics, or to make soothing promises of imminent change, than to engage the outside world in the free and non-manipulative dialogue

Japan so urgently needs with all of its international partners. American lawyers have been stymied in their earlier hopes of helping U.S. firms enter the Japanese market; foreign correspondents are systematically walled off from their most important sources; resident Western and Asian academics in search of stable and productive careers find the roads blocked; students from abroad are trapped in their own little boxes; and foreign scientists and engineers are kept out of the loop at Japan's state-of-the-art laboratories. Intellectual parsimony on such a grand scale is simply not worthy of the world's second economic power as it seeks a permanent seat on the Security Council and aspires to political leadership at the regional and global levels.

Indeed, far from enhancing cultural relations or "mutual understanding," these cages for foreign intellectuals—some of them gilded, most of them not—cost Japan dearly in the resentment and mistrust they engender among such individuals, their Tokyo embassies, and their home governments. As Japan's conservative forces tout their new slogan of a "Normal Country,"[2]—a code word, in fact, for little other than building up Japan's military in the name of making a greater "international contribution" in peacekeeping operations and regional security— one must ask how a powerful nation maintaining a closed market and society can by any stretch of the imagination be called "normal" or seen as "contributing" to the world's weal.

Meanwhile, the United States, by failing to push now for the dismantling of Japan's cartels of the mind, risks their eventual export to the rest of Asia in a rolling emulation effect. Once again, Uncle Sam's foreign policy bark has been stronger than his bite.

In the name of open markets and democracy the first Clinton administration committed the nation to a continuing economic, cultural, and military presence in East Asia, including the maintenance of present troop levels through the year 2015. This costly strategic ante ultimately depends on credible progress in the other two sectors, above all greater access to Asia's booming markets. American voters, anxious now above all for their own pocketbooks and no longer recruitable for unwinnable ground wars in Asia, will see to that. Yet Washington's efforts to prod its chief and most advanced partner in the region toward free trade have had all the chomp of an ageing cocker spaniel—something that has not been lost on other Asian nations increasingly inclined to take their lead from Japan.

An unrestricted discourse and intellectual presence are essential for the successful pursuit of America's economic and political objectives in East Asia. That Japan's intellectual protectionism has so long been overlooked stems variously from the long nonchalant decades of preponderant U.S. power; from the fact that market goods like apples, automobiles, and semiconductors are easier to get excited over and quantify in terms of their economic impact; and because the American professionals who struggle against these obstacles in Japan seldom look beyond their own parochial quandary to the strikingly similar restrictions in other fields. While loudly proclaiming what we take to be our universal values of free trade, democracy, and human rights, we pragmatic Americans tend to be impatient with the more subtly nuanced institutional and psychological factors in our dialogue with other nations. Our difficulties in dealing with the Islamic world have been better dramatized, but this mental impatience (if we may call it that) and lack of intellectual sophistication have been particularly costly to the United States in its relationship with Japan.

Nearly three decades of work with Japanese intellectuals, most of it in Japan, have convinced me of the need for an extended look at Japan's cartels of the mind, and I have drawn as appropriate on my own professional experience for illustration and authentication of the argument. During the 1960s I was a Harvard doctoral candidate in modern Japanese history, one of that younger generation of Western scholars who were seeking fresher and more positive "takes" on Japan following all those depressing if essential studies from the 1950s as to what had "gone wrong" during the prewar period. Throughout the early 1970s I was active in Tokyo in a number of capacities that broadened my contacts with Japanese intellectuals beyond those I had enjoyed with academic mentors and fellow scholars while in Japan as a dissertation researcher from 1966 to 1969. These included brief periods of service as the Japan correspondent for the now defunct *Philadelphia Bulletin* and *Washington Star*; as a consultant to the International Association for Cultural Freedom and the Harvard-Yenching Institute (a fund at Harvard for the promotion of ties with scholars in East Asia); and as the Japan representative for Harvard's successful $8.5 million fund drive in Japan in support of Japanese Studies at the university.

My duties as a correspondent and academic representative during these years also put me in touch with scholars and "public intellectuals" in Korea, Taiwan, Hong Kong, and Southeast Asia, which built in turn on my earlier service in the South Asian region as an assistant cultural attaché for the United States Information Service at the American embassy in Kabul, Afghanistan, and at our consulate general in Dhaka, Bangladesh (then still Dacca, East Pakistan), during 1958–1961. Having long viewed Japan from Asia as well as from the West, I have tried to avoid that *folie à deux* obsession with the bilateral tie that, from good will or ill, so often engulfs the American specialist on Japan.

As the first Associate Director and Japan Representative of the newly created Japan–United States Friendship Commission, a minuscule federal agency for funding cultural exchanges with Japan, I was active from 1977 to 1984 in negotiating a wide spectrum of new exchange programs with Japanese universities, theaters, museums, media organizations, and educational officials. Finally, from 1984 to 1993 I taught Japanese students as a professor at three of Japan's better-known universities—Tsukuba, Keio, and Gakushuin—and at the latter was fully integrated into the teaching and administrative duties of the Japanese faculty, giving six undergraduate and graduate courses on American and Japanese intellectual history, international cultural relations, and political thought, all but one of them taught in Japanese.

Throughout this third of a century of contact with Japan and its intellectuals, I have been blessed with warm friendships, continuous mental stimulation, and the pleasantness of living in a society virtually free of violent crime, low in anti-intellectualism, and high in an outward decorum that would have gladdened my Victorian grandmothers. To top it all, there have been the cultural riches of Tokyo—the only global megalopolis combining a hi-tech urban lifestyle with an orientation that is equally toward Asia and the West. Although the following pages pull no punches as to certain features of Japanese intellectual life, neither this book nor its author should be construed as being "anti-Japanese"—any more than an account, say, of racial discrimination in the United States by a Japanese writer should be automatically tarred with the brush of "anti-Americanism." Nor is this volume intended as a comprehensive report card on Japan. As too often happens, some Japanese readers (or foreign Japanophiles) may choose to take it as a blanket criticism, but it is merely a deep probe into one special yet very important aspect of the country.

For reasons of space my argument has largely been confined to the Japan-U.S. axis, although in many cases the problems I deal with here apply equally to Japan's intellectual contacts with Europe and Asia.

In recent years some American scholars, journalists, and public intellectuals have been reluctant to write in a critical vein about Japan for fear of somehow offending the Japanese. Their retreat into self-censorship further reflects the American mood of the mid-1990s. Indeed, when not temporarily reassured by the latest dip in the Tokyo Stock Exchange, many Americans still find themselves ill at ease with Japan.

It's not just that we feel vaguely threatened by the growing global trading and financial clout of the Japanese, including their aggressive and free-handed reach into our own economy—their ability to buy into our land and industries and financial institutions, to establish a major presence in American universities and research centers, and to lobby our legislators or even influence our presidential elections to their own advantage. More unnerving and exasperating has been our failure—despite years of entreaty and table-thumping—to get Tokyo to reciprocate the favor by opening up its own market and society and cultural institutions to the rest of world.

Why doesn't Japan, given its newfound power and the responsibilities that presumably go with it, act with a bit more *noblesse oblige*? Why can't the Japanese respond in the expected fashion to the rational claims of mutuality in an increasingly interdependent world? Why don't they begin to repay in part the benefits they have reaped over the past half-century from the economic, social, and intellectual access their country has had to the rest of the industrialized world? Why does Japan—140 years after Perry, 50 years after V-J Day, and going into the twenty-first century—still keep itself so tightly shut?

Unfortunately, the outside world's study and understanding of how Japan's "hard-core" bureaucratic, political, and industrial mechanisms operate to keep its economy closed have progressed more rapidly than our comprehension of Japan's intellectual, emotional, and cultural postures toward others—the "soft-core" lining of Japan's social insularity. We still fail to see most of what is going on at these levels, and what little we do see we usually fail to understand, thereby heightening our own sense of bafflement and anxiety. I am not referring here to those panoramic portraits of the Japanese mind and culture on which whole libraries have been written, but to the more limited but critical area of perceptions, assumptions, motivations, ideological constructs, and institutional arrangements that govern the way the Japanese see themselves in relation to the rest of international society. Non-Japanese, for a variety of reasons, balk at a serious exploration of the attitudes propping up Japan's intellectual barriers toward the world outside, not least because so much of what one turns up seems so downright preposterous. Americans have difficulty focusing on this dimension of Japan because of our own ethnocentric universalism, which assumes that people everywhere are basically alike, i.e., like us. Europeans remain blinded by their sheer intellectual hauteur. Other Asians, the historical victims of Japanese nationalism, hang back due to their deep-seated wariness, cynicism, and sense of *déjà vu*.

None of this should imply that the outsider in Japan makes no friends or has no fun, or that, for the well-heeled, safely ghettoized, and nonthreatening Caucasian expatriate, Tokyo cannot still be just this side of paradise. This book, however, is not about personal paradises lost or regained, but about a basic aspect of Japan today. Japanese insularity and the denial of reciprocity that it engenders are *important*—not only for individuals, professions, and industries, but for the greater national interest of the United States or that of any other nation engaged with Japan. By the same token, it is precisely because they have decided that Japanese insularity is *not* important that so many Americans and others repeatedly play the dupe to it.

As the eminent scholar and translator Edward Seidensticker, a perceptive and dry-eyed observer of contemporary Japan, put it some time ago:

> I have recently felt that I might be getting mellow. . . . The Japanese are just like other people. They work hard to support their—but no. They are not like everyone else. They are infinitely more clannish, insular, parochial, and one owes it to one's self-respect to preserve a certain outrage at the insularity. To have the sense of outrage go dull is to lose the will to communicate; and that I think is death. So I am going home.[3]

From the nineteenth-century author Lafcadio Hearn down to Walter Mondale, America's ambassador to Japan from 1993 to 1996, foreigners in Japan who deal with the Japanese in any depth eventually butt their heads against that parochial wall. It was that same clannishness of Japanese scholars, writers, and other intellectuals that infuriated the initially enchanted Hearn and Seidensticker, eight decades apart. For Mondale (unwilling to be taken in like his predecessor Mike Mansfield), it was the "hard lesson" he learned during his first half year in Tokyo— about the intractability of Japanese trade barriers and the arguments used to defend them. As 1993 gave way to 1994 this awakening brought on a "complete reversal," from pliant to tough, in the tone of the U.S. ambassador's advice to Washington.[4] Within months of his arrival he surprised a group of American corporate officials by "jerking a clenched fist upward in a gesture of disgust," to say of Japan's officials: "they're f—— us."[5] More startling than the expletive was the emergence at long last of an American envoy who actually saw what was going on, and cared.

For those who want (and need) to understand or grapple with Japan's insular mentality, the personal honesty of a Seidensticker—the refusal to shun outrage—is the beginning of wisdom. The broader aim of this book, however, is to expose the institutional structures, ideological defenses, and practical consequences of Japan's "cartels of the mind," and to examine some of the fitful and ineffective attempts to challenge them in the past. By so doing, I also hope to encourage other foreign scholars, politicians, business people, journalists, and public intellectuals—not only from America but around the world—to follow the intellectual and political honesty of a Mondale in refusing the often beguiling awards (financial, professional, political, or ego-boosting, as the case may be) of continued self-delusion.

(On a consequent point of style: It is precisely with such general readers in mind that I beg the indulgence of the professional Japan specialist for my omission of line-cluttering macrons to indicate Japanese double vowels, and for my rendering of Japanese personal names in the English sequence, surname last.)

Cartels of the Mind

1

LEGAL LANDING
The Attorneys' Narrow Beachhead

The practical catalogue of Japanese exclusionism and xeno-phobia is well documented and widely known. At the "harder" end of the spectrum stand those impersonal, economic market barriers that constrain the entry of foreign goods and investment—bureaucratic regulations, the non-transparent "administrative guidance" to private corporations, or the col-lusive bidding system of the construction industry known as *dango*. At the "softer" end we find noneconomic, often poignantly personal, barriers that verge on racial discrimi-nation—the refusal to rent apartments to foreign students, the debarring from national high-school sports contests of third-generation Japan-born Korean youngsters, or the way in which American baseball and sumo stars in Japan have been deliber-ately tripped up just short of reaching the highest honors.

The obstacles to foreign products reflect a rationally chosen and politically dictated mercantilist economic policy, while the curbs on foreign people are the product of nonrational yet deeply ingrained antiforeign sentiment. There is, nevertheless, a wide conceptual and attitudinal overlap between the two sorts of barriers. Mercantilism not only protects the market, but it also serves to maintain cultural purity and unsullied social ways by keeping the foreign business population to a fraction of the

Japanese trading communities now resident in major Western and Asian cities. Conversely, xenophobia toward foreigners in Japan derives not only from anxiety about the social and cultural order but also from a hardheaded motivation among individual Japanese to limit the economic and professional competition.

At the junction of mercantilist-style institutional barriers and attitudinal xenophobia lie the severe professional restrictions placed upon foreign lawyers, journalists, and academics working for the long term in Japan—restrictions that do not apply to their Japanese counterparts active in the West. Similar obstacles encumber foreign students and scientific researchers who are in Japan for a shorter time. As purveyors of information and ideas, foreigners in these five categories provide Japan with its most direct and personal mode of intellectual contact with the outside world—as opposed to what the Japanese read in books or are told by their political and media leaders. These are the "markets" that will have to be "liberalized" before the U.S. or other nations can hope to have a genuinely open and effective dialogue with the Japanese people.

Oddly, these barriers, all from time to time reported and deplored, have been little understood collectively as a possible clue to Japan's overall behavior and intentions as a global power. The prospects for a more open society, for the healthy development of Japan's democratic institutions, for a firm refusal to retread the old militarist path, and for a constructive role in Asia, will all be reduced to the extent that this exclusionist mentality is allowed to persist. Unfortunately, our own failure to challenge these barriers virtually assures their continuity.

The case of foreign lawyers has become a trade issue proper, and they have enjoyed the strongest support from their own governments since their ability to practice in Japan could help foreign corporations penetrate the Japanese market. Foreign correspondents, backed by their home offices and sympathetic embassies, have also been able to make minor inroads against the entrenched Japanese system. Foreign professors, working as they do within Japanese institutions, are the most exposed to

systematic discrimination and have received the least help from
the outside.

The ordeals of the foreign legal, media, and academic professions in Japan have all followed a depressingly similar pattern:

1. We start with Japanese systems that are of course somewhat different from those found in the West, the contrasts usually being greatest with America, since prewar Japan had borrowed many of its institutions from Europe (especially Germany).
2. At their point of contact with the outside world these systems have been systematically closed to direct and equal participation by foreign professionals. Before Japan's takeoff as a major economic power, however, little attention was paid to these barriers—indeed, during the early postwar decades the few foreign professionals in Tokyo rather enjoyed their segregated status as feted, exotic outsiders, living at a material level of comfort well above that of their Japanese counterparts.
3. From the 1970s, however, the outside world began to demand reciprocal access for foreign professionals commensurate with Japan's global economic influence and the opportunities Japan's professionals had long been enjoying in the West.
4. This inaugurated a tedious process over a quarter century—far from finished today—whereby sporadic foreign pressures have been grudgingly met by glacially incremental Japanese concessions.
5. Tokyo's defensive arguments have focused on cultural exceptionalism and on the technical difficulties that allegedly stand in the way of rapid liberalization. Here, four players are typically involved: the foreign protagonists seeking access; a minority of Japanese supporting the foreigners' cause out of a concern for Japan's external relations; the majority of the Japanese in each respective field determined to guard their own turf; and a minuscule group of foreign apologists who stand with the Japanese on their ramparts. Over all this activity lies a smokescreen of Japanese promises of "internationalization"

(*kokusaika*) and the pall of a seemingly incurable self-delusion among the foreign protagonists that the Japanese side intends, in due time, to permit a genuine opening.

HALF A FOOT INSIDE THE DOOR

The 18 July 1992 issue of the *Economist* described Japan's tight numerical restrictions on its own lawyers and judges as the "first component of a potent cartel." Because of this "lawyers' cartel," the journal continued, the scarcity and high price of lawyers and the delays in the court system compel many Japanese to seek redress by other means. The chances of justice, however, are stacked against individual litigants in out-of-court negotiations when powerful corporate respondents know there is little credible threat of being hauled before a judge.

By the early 1990s Japanese critics, too, were complaining of a "cartel" that restricted competition and the servicing of citizens' legal needs both by means of the excessively severe entry requirements to the lawyers' "guild,"[1] and by its minimum-fee schedules, arguably in violation of Japan's antitrust legislation.[2] The third major device in maintaining the lawyers' cartel—and our concern here—has been the barring of foreign attorneys from all but a minimal presence in Japan.

Although my purpose is to illuminate the external consequences of these cartels of the mind rather than attempt a full institutional description of Japan's intellectual industries per se, each enterprise deserves a brief setting.

Japan's door to foreign legal professionals has been kept closed, except for a crack, by an artificially limited elite of litigation lawyers, known as *bengoshi*, and the all-powerful, autonomous Japan Federation of Bar Associations (JFBA: the Nihon Bengoshi Rengokai, or Nichibenren for short) to which they all must belong. The needle's eye through which they all have passed is the entrance examination for the Supreme Court's Legal Research and Training Institute (Shiho Kenshujo). Although often referred to as Japan's "only law school," the LRTI as a single exclusive national institution is more like Annapolis or West Point. After sitting an average of six to seven times for its annual admission test, about 700 of Japan's future legal elite (out of an annual applicant pool that had risen to 24,423 by 1995) enter the LRTI each year at the average age of 28. The rate of those passing the test in recent years has been in the range of 2.5 to 3 percent, in contrast to the almost 50 percent pass rate for American bar exams depending on the state giving the test. After a two-year course including 16 months of apprenticeship with district courts, public prosecutors' offices, and practicing lawyers, approximately 600 of the annual graduates of the LRTI become *bengoshi*, while over 70 them are selected as judges (*hanji*) and about 50 go to work as public prosecutors (*kenji*).[3]

The misleading (if typical) equating by Japan's Economic Planning Agency of the 14,433 *bengoshi* registered in 1991 (one for every 8,569 Japanese citizens) with 700,000 U.S. "lawyers" in 1990 (one for every 356 Americans) is the sort of comparison that has bolstered the oversimplified image of Japan as a non-litigious society.[4] In fact, the *bengoshi* (who numbered 15,538 by 1995) function more like trial attorneys in America or barristers in Britain. For the most part narrowly trained specialists in criminal defense and civil litigation, they represent merely the apex of a much larger pyramid of over 130,000 registered professionals providing legal services in Japan, nearly all of whom would go by the name of "lawyer" in the U.S. As of 1990, in addition to the then 14,173 *bengoshi*, 2,017 judges, and 1,173 public prosecutors who were graduates of the LRTI, there were 16,488 judicial scriveners (known as *shiho shoshi*), who prepare complaints for individuals representing themselves in court and advise on disputes involving inheritance and real estate; 34,764 administrative scriveners (*gyosei shoshi*), who draft petitions and advise clients who have problems with government agencies or licensing bureaus; 56,624 tax attorneys (*zeirishi*); and 3,342 patent attorneys (*benrishi*).

All of these Japanese "paralegal" professionals have taken stringent national exams in their specialized fields, some of them with pass rates as stiff as those of the LRTI, and they perform work that in the U.S. could only be done by licensed attorneys. By contrast, Japan's estimated 10,500 corporate in-house legal advisers (roughly corresponding to American corporate counsel or to Britain's solicitors) and its 2,000-some government in-house legal advisers (similarly drawn from the permanent staff, and the closest thing to a U.S. government lawyer) come to their jobs with no more formal preparation than a university bachelor's degree from an undergraduate law faculty (*hogakubu*). These "law" faculties typically offer a European-style mix of law, public administration, and political science, with a coverage of legal codes and principles sufficient for the provision of general, back-office counseling services. This represents the same basic academic legal background as that of the *bengoshi* prior to entering the LRTI—where most of the time is spent in practical on-the-job training. Japan's 2,500 law professors, after five years of teaching in a *hogakubu*, may become *bengoshi* without attending the LRTI, although most prefer to remain in academe.

Finally, in a striking point too rarely noted, Japan possesses a strongly law-oriented, legalistically trained cadre in its higher bureaucrats, government negotiators, and policymakers, the cream of whom were among the 30,000 students Japan graduates annually from these undergraduate law faculties. They bring to their work a more narrowly focused intellectual background, and a greater national-interest-oriented zeal, than do their American counterparts, most of whom have had a broadly based liberal arts education as well as some private-sector experience.[5]

Japan's elitist and highly compartmentalized pyramid of legal practitioners contrasts with the widely recruited, broadly trained, and subsequently specializing American profession, where bar-exam failures are the result of undershooting a qualitative standard rather than of a politically dictated *numerus clausus*. Other differences reflect Japan's essential character as an administrative state that favors the discretion of judges, the explication of comprehensive legal codes, low settlement awards, and a bureaucratically-minded tilt toward social order—as opposed to America's celebration of juries, citizens' rights, lavish compensation sums, and the rhetorical skills of flamboyant trial attorneys pushing forward the boundaries of case law.

Japan's legal system, like that of continental Europe, is based on civil law, rather than on the common law tradition of Britain and America. The continuing influence of the German model, introduced during the Meiji period (1868–1912), is seen in the bias toward extreme judicial intervention and fragmentation and in the learning of general legal principles, with little of the Anglo-Saxon emphasis on developing adversarial forensic skills and applying them to concrete situations. Law "offices" in Japan tend to be small compared to U.S. law "firms," and are structured as cooperatives rather than as American-style partnerships where the firm itself is a legal entity that assumes the risk for the work of its members. Each *bengoshi* is responsible for his own legal opinions. Most of them work as solo practitioners, and Japanese law offices with more than ten members are rare, in contrast to the several hundred lawyers employed by the larger U.S. firms.

Whereas American lawyers are supervised by the courts and are not required to join bar associations, Japanese *bengoshi* are required to belong to the JFBA (Nichibenren), which supervises the profession independently of the Ministry of Justice (Homusho). Brought into being under the Occupation to guarantee the independence of the *bengoshi* newly freed from the smothering embrace of the prewar justice ministry, the Federation's virtually total autonomy has enabled it to resist broader government calls for liberalization. In a historical irony that we shall see repeated in the cases of Japan's postwar press and universities, the powerful reaction to prewar and wartime government controls ended up creating new pockets of vested professional interests, jealously defended in liberty's name, that present continuing barriers to foreign participation today.

There was little push by foreign lawyers for entry into Japan's legal market until the mid-1970s and early 1980s, when bank deregulation and the sharp rise in the yen brought Tokyo to the fore as the world's third financial capital after New York and London. Eager for a piece of the action, America's powerful and globally networked international law firms ran into adamant opposition from the small but growing number of *bengoshi* who specialized in international corporate law (about six to seven hundred of them by 1994) and who were determined to protect the most lucrative niche in Japanese lawyering. While some Japanese academics argued that the practice of foreign law in Japan should be unregulated, there was no effective challenge to the JFBA's position that its monopoly on legal services in Japan extended to the international sector. The fight was on. There are five watershed dates for foreign lawyers in postwar Japan: 1949, 1955, 1977, 1986, and 1994.

During the Occupation, 73 foreign lawyers, most of them American, were licensed to practice under Article 7 of the new Lawyers Law (Bengoshi Ho) of 1949, 57 of them registering with local bar associations as *junkaiin* (associate members). It was assumed by the Japanese government that they would automatically bring in more foreign business, and by U.S. officials that they would introduce an American-style legal climate that would contribute to the growth of Japanese democracy. Both assumptions were wide of the mark, but the *junkaiin* did demonstrate that there were no ineffable "cultural differences" preventing American and Japanese lawyers from working together effectively as professional colleagues in the same firm, if only the regulations would allow them to do so.

Some of the Americans had trained a number of today's leading Japanese international lawyers, but by 1955, with Japan asserting its recently won independence, there was a reaction against any further foreign tutelage. Article 7 was deleted, thereby effectively excluding foreign lawyers and law firms from the Japanese market except for the (today virtually extinct) *junkaiin*, who were grandfathered by supplementary provisions and allowed to retain their monopoly as the sole foreigners in the legal business until a new foreign lawyers' law was passed in 1986. For three decades the only work in Japan available to incoming foreign lawyers (mostly younger expatriates) was as "trainees" or "legal consultants" to Japanese law firms or corporations doing chores normally reserved for legal assistants, such as the drafting of English-language agreements and the research and proofreading of documents. Under pain of prison they were forbidden to advise on, let alone litigate under, Japanese law, and the JFBA cautioned the Japanese international law firms hiring such foreign "trainees" not to keep them for more than two or three years—lest, presumably, they might become too familiar with Japanese law and legal practice and develop into a source of future competition. (We shall encounter this resistance to the longer-staying, seriously acculturating, foreign professional most strikingly in the case of foreign scholars, in Chapter 3.)

By the late 1970s, amid all the new slogans about *kokusaika*, or "internationalization," pressure for liberalizing the legal market was coming from the Japanese Foreign Ministry (Gaimusho) and from business circles including the powerful Federation of Economic Organizations (Keidanren). The diplomats were concerned about Japan's image abroad, the economic leaders about the efficient legal servicing of Japan's swelling overseas trade and investment activities. Despite such influential supporters, Isaac Shapiro of New York's Milbank Tweed was threatened with jail when he came to Tokyo to open the first foreign law office in 1977 on the strength of a special bureaucratic dispensation. In response to the strident protest from the JFBA the visa applications from all other foreign firms were shelved for another decade. The American Bar Association had first approached Japan for access in 1974, but the issue remained stalled until 1982, when it was taken up by the U.S. Trade Representative and made an integral part of the U.S. government's market-opening negotiations. That led, after many pressures and complaints—and in a pattern typical of the other professional areas—to the very limited toehold granted by the Foreign Lawyers Special Act of 1986. This was followed, after nearly another decade of renewed negotiations, by the amendments of 1994, which were little more than cosmetic embellishments on the originally minimal concessions.

Spurred on by Prime Minister Yasuhiro Nakasone's inclusion of legal services in his promised market-opening "package" of 1985, and by threats of retaliation under Section 301 of the 1974 Trade Act from U.S. Trade Representative Clayton Yeutter, the new legislation of 1986 restricted American lawyers to advising on American law. That opened up the limited (though very lucrative) business of assisting Japanese firms with their penetration of the U.S. economy through acquisitions, mergers, and other investments, and by defending them in American courts against accusations of dumping or discriminatory hiring policies. But U.S. lawyers were barred from the reciprocal function of expediting market penetration and investments by American business in Japan—something that disappointed both the American business community in Japan and the U.S. government, which had viewed this as the main reason for backing the demands for professional access.

Facilitating the interests of U.S. corporations in Japan's market requires counsel on Japanese law, something that the *bengoshi* were best capable of supplying. The new 1986 law, however, placed the entire area of advice and litigation on Japanese law beyond the reach of foreign law firms. This was achieved by prohibiting foreign lawyers from forming partnerships with *bengoshi* or hiring them as associates with a guaranteed salary—although Japanese law firms, as we have seen, have been free all along to hire foreign law consultants. This ban on tapping the expertise of Japanese lawyers directly, as members of a foreign law firm, makes it impossible for foreign law firms to provide efficient and comprehensive "one-stop" service to their clients. Maintained over strong foreign protest in the minor amendments to the law in 1994, this restriction continues to be the main grievance of American lawyers in Japan today.

In a bizarre corollary to that ban, Japanese *bengoshi* who have gone on to pass an American bar exam, joined an American law firm in the U.S., and have subsequently been repatriated by that firm to its Tokyo office, must surrender their *bengoshi* status while in Japan and may function only as "foreign" lawyers—in their own country. That is what happened to Tsunemasa Terai, who graduated from the LRTI in the 1970s after finishing high in his class at Keio University. He practiced law in Japan for three years, received a U.S. law degree from Michigan, was admitted to the New York bar, and returned to Tokyo as a partner with Cleary, Gottlieb, Steen & Hamilton in 1991. Under the limitations of the 1986 law, which had been heralded as "opening" the profession to outsiders, foreign lawyers could offer counsel only on the laws of their home country or state. In the name of "reciprocity" only Americans from U.S. jurisdictions that had adopted rules for practice by foreign lawyers—i.e., for those who had not passed a local American bar, and were technically classified as Foreign Legal

Consultants (FLCs)—could be licensed in Japan. The offering of advice on third-country law, and counsel in international arbitration, were ruled out altogether.

As of 1986 the eight jurisdictions were Alaska, California, Hawaii, the District of Columbia, Illinois, Michigan, New York, and Washington. By 1996 another fourteen states had been added, and as part of the GATT services framework (and in line with Most Favored Nation rules) Japan agreed to permit waivers of its strict reciprocity rules by the Minister of Justice on a case-by-case basis.

Other restrictions in the 1986 law were more in the nature of procedural nuisances designed, it seemed, to buttress the formalistic contention by the JFBA that foreign firms should not be permitted to practice Japanese law because the firms themselves were *not present* in Japan and would therefore escape the necessary supervision. This was an extraordinary bit of sophistry inasmuch as the firms' representatives were considered present enough by Japanese tax and immigration authorities and had been screened by, and required to register with, the JFBA. In a gesture of deliberate denigration, foreign lawyers were not permitted to hang out the shingle of their home firms, but could identify their offices only by their personal names, followed by their official designation as *gaikokuho jimu bengoshi* (*gaiben* for short).

"*Gaikokuho bengoshi*," literally a "foreign-law attorney," should have been enough, but, in a patent ploy to peg the foreigners at a lower status level, the deprecatory modifier "*jimu*"—which has the nuance of "clerical"—was also inserted. *Jimu bengoshi* is the the term used for British solicitors, and the "business" connoted by *jimu* is simply mundane *office* business, not the glamorous *corporate* "business" suggested by the Western media's hopeful mistranslation of the title as "foreign business lawyer." The implication was that foreign lawyers were not true *bengoshi*, not professional equals, but merely some sort of specialized technicians. Finally, the requirement for at least five years' practical experience in the country of origin after qualifying as an attorney disqualified most of the foreign legal "trainees" at Japanese firms and others with previous experience in Japan. This was especially resented by those young Tokyo-based lawyers who had to return home after having made a heavy investment in Japanese language and legal studies and committed themselves to careers as Japan specialists.[6]

American disappointment with the limited opening of 1986 ran deep, and in October 1989 U.S. Trade Representative Carla Hills requested a new round of trade talks. Japan's restrictions on foreign lawyers were cited as a non-tariff barrier in the 1989 National Trade Estimate Report on Trade Barriers, raising the possibility of retaliatory action under the Super 301 section of the new Trade Act. In December of 1993 the issue was included at the last minute under service industries by the U.S. GATT negotiating team in Geneva. There, in an ironic twist, the deputy USTR chief John Schmidt—in an alleged tradeoff for Japanese restriction of patent flooding on semiconductors—accepted the very limited Japanese offer for "joint enterprises" that the American Bar Association and America's *gaiben* in Tokyo had been strenuously opposing. "We've lost ten years' worth of progress," lamented White & Case's Robert F. Grondine, chairman of the Legal Services Committee of the American Chamber of Commerce in Japan, who together with the USTR's Japan staff had been pushing for a genuinely meaningful deal, or none at all.[7]

Once again, the Japanese mountain had labored with fresh recommendations from the prime minister's council on administrative reform and a joint JFBA-Ministry of Justice study committee. Once again, in predictable deference to the JFBA's stand-pattism, it gave birth to another mouse. Removing minor irritants, the amended law of 1994 allowed foreign lawyers to post the name of their parent firm on their office portals and calling cards, and accepted two years' work in Japan as part of the five years' practical-experience requirement. The questions of standing in international arbitration and of competency in third-country law (and other multijurisdictional transactions where the globally connected *gaiben* enjoy enormous advantages) were not addressed. (In late 1996, by further amendment of the law, foreign lawyers were finally allowed to represent clients of all nationalities in international arbitrations in Japan.) And the two key foreign demands for partnerships with and the hiring of Japanese associates were circumvented by the proferring of a progressive-sounding but virtually unworkable device known as the "joint enterprise" (*kyodo jigyo*).

This was in essence little more than a space-sharing arrangement designed to ensure the hermetic separation of the participating Japanese and foreign law firms. Neither a single nor a joint legal entity, the "joint enterprise" was a juridical zombie—the sort of fleeting contractual joint venture that, for example, two construction companies enter into for cooperating in the erection of a new building. Lawyers from the Japanese side are not permitted to have any connection with the foreign parent firm, and can share only those revenues and expenses arising from joint operations in Japan—which has left them with little incentive to tie up with foreign firms.[8] Advice on Japanese law and third-country legal matters remains the exclusive prerogative of the Japanese *bengoshi* in the joint venture, and Japanese litigation has to be handled outside the joint venture altogether by the Japanese law office.

By 1995 only two out of the approximately 45 foreign law firms in Tokyo had snapped up this crumb of concession and entered into such an arrangement. Not only was there no meaningful expansion of permissible activity under a "joint enterprise," but the JFBA notification requirements seemed ominously intrusive to the foreign firms. The clincher for Americans was the impossibility, under this amorphous arrangement, of meeting the stricter U.S. ethical standards on conflicts of interest or attorney-client privilege. On the one hand, it would be impossible to check out potential conflicts of interest among mutual clients without full access to the Japanese firm's files; on the other, the confidentiality of clients and of information relating to them would be vunerable to inadvertent disclosure where two independent firms share office space, library resources, and clerical staff.

CULTURAL AND TECHNICAL RATIONALES FOR DEBARMENT

Both the mindset and the broader purposes at work behind these continuing restrictions are best revealed by the rhetoric used by the Japanese side to defend them. The culturalist arguments are basically three: that Japan's purportedly nonlitigious society will be corrupted by combative American "over-lawyering"; that Japan's small-scale law offices and nascent international law practice will be swamped by America's mammoth, well-heeled law firms, which will siphon off Japan's brightest young lawyers with their higher salaries; and that the U.S., by seeking to impose its own legal traditions on Japan, is in fact practicing a form of cultural imperialism. The technical defenses center on the Americans' not having qualified under Japan's "bar exam" for the LRTI, and on the alleged lack of reciprocity *for Japanese in the U.S.*

During the debate leading up to the 1986 law, Junjiro Tsubota (who holds an LL.M. from Harvard Law School and specializes in international transactions with a Japanese firm in Tokyo) noted the objective, system-related fact that, since Japan's courts rely mainly on comprehensive civil law codes that offer relatively little opportunity for legal maneuvering, Japanese attorneys are reluctant to file suits on speculation, that is, where they see a less than fifty percent chance of winning. This naturally limits the possibility of spectacular monetary judgments and, with that, the temptation to canvass aggressively for clients simply on the chance of reaping a financial bonanza. Tsubota went further, however, to paint the standard subjective, culture-bound image of Japanese lawyering:

> . . . when people act in good faith, and honor even vague oral promises, few things are litigated. People don't much care if their agreements are legally binding or even if there are loopholes allowing for opportunistic behavior. In a *nonlitigious society*, where *commercial reasonableness* prevails, it would be crazy to hire lawyers and spend large sums of money on legal paperwork. [emphasis added][9]

These idyllic self-images of Japan's legal culture (pinpointed in my italics) are bolstered by the tendency to take as an achieved fact the normative injunction to Japanese lawyers, in the opening words of the Lawyers Law of 1949, that their mission is to "protect fundamental human rights and realize social justice."[10]

Indeed, as Shirohei Hashimoto, then secretary-general of the JFBA, put it grandly to a newspaper reporter in 1987:

> Legal practice is a respectable profession, dedicated to social justice and upholding human rights. . . . In America, however, legal practice seems to be more of a business in the service sector than a lofty ideal.[11]

Japanese *bengoshi* were incensed at having their profession lumped together with grapefruits and automobiles as an object of trade negotiations. In fact, however, *bengoshi* are among Japan's most highly paid professionals, with an average take-home pay in 1990 of 15,440,000 yen, over $106,000 at the then yen rate of 145 to the dollar—a sum that would have exceeded $188,000 at the mid-1995 rate of 82 to 1.[12] And Japan's international lawyers generally are found near the top of the pay scale.

That did not stop Akira Kawamura, the chairman of the JFBA Foreign Lawyers Committee in 1994, from embellishing on the somewhat precious collective self-image when he wrote:

> In Japan lawyers rarely participate in business activities but strictly preserve their professional integrity by limiting their scope to legal practice and serving the public in human rights causes. Japanese lawyers now concede that the commercial behavior of large law firms means that foreign lawyers function in quite a different way from Japanese.[13]

With Tokyo's two largest law offices counting no more than 51 *bengoshi* apiece as of 1994, as compared to 1,604 and 1,170 in the two most heavily staffed U.S. firms, the Japanese may have an understandable sense of inferiority when it comes to numbers. But the deeper anxiety seems to be that the more aggressive, protean, and globally networked American firms will not only take the cream of Japan's more ambitious young lawyers, but also allow Japanese who fail the LRTI exam but enter American practice through "easy" U.S. law schools and bar exams to reenter Japan through the back door as "foreign lawyers."

Kawamura expressed his further fear that "the sheer strength of capital and human resources would unduly influence the host country's legal market and judicial system," projecting his anxieties beyond Japan to warn that, "Domination of Anglo-American legal practice in areas such as Asia and Asia Pacific will not benefit the societies involved."[14] Or, as Kunio Hamada of Hamada & Matsumoto (Tokyo) put it, even more bluntly: "There is no question American lawyers seek the hegemony of American jurisprudence around the world."[15]

"(The) Japanese legal profession sees itself as defending public interests and protecting individuals' rights and many view the corporate bias of U.S. law firms as conflicting with these interests," intoned a Japanese study group's report to the Ministry of Justice in 1993. "The big issue," it concluded, "is not whether Japan is practicing unfair trade by not accepting U.S. law firms on American terms, but whether the world should adapt to the Anglo-U.S. system." By puffing up the issue to one of planetary hegemony, and by calling for a multilaterally negotiated "global standard," the study group hit upon the perfect device for putting off any bilateral improvements indefinitely.[16]

What we have here as a rationale for circumscribing the activities of foreign lawyers in Japan—and, as we shall see, of journalists and scholars, too—is an overkill of sociocultural theorizing, aggravated by a penchant for inflating the limited contact or competition between actual principals—in this case between Japanese and American international corporate lawyers—to a cultural confrontation between two whole societies, or between the international corporate branch of American lawyering and the entire Japanese legal tradition.

In fact there are only a few outer sprockets of the two national legal systems that are actually meshing—let alone sparking with "cultural friction." Japan's local bar has simply not been inundated by a rush of excess lawyers from the U.S., nor has Japan been pressed by foreign law firms into becoming a more litigious society. By 1994 about 30 U.S. law firms, 15 from the U.K., and one each from France, Germany, and the Netherlands had opened offices in Japan, with a stable plateau of 70 to 80 *gaiben*—as against more than 15,000 *bengoshi*—registered in Japan during the years 1991–1994. About two-thirds of these were American, most of the others British. That fell far short of the hundreds that were originally predicted, and agonized over, by the JFBA. With the luster now off Japan's economy and its financial markets, it is unlikely that the number of *gaiben* will increase significantly in the foreseeable future. Indeed, there were five foreign law firms that closed their Tokyo offices in 1994–1995, and as of late 1995 the number of registered foreign lawyers had fallen to between 65 and 70. Even in the late 1980s, at the height of Japan's "bubble economy," when the outlanders first began arriving, the costs and logistical difficulties of stationing American staff in Tokyo put a severe cap on their numbers—what with operational expenses averaging $2 million a year, secretarial salaries running the equivalent of a young lawyer's pay back home, the drawbacks of expatriate schooling for children, and the ambitious lawyer's reluctance to remain outside the home office "loop" too long.

Indeed, the greatest beneficiaries of the influx have been Japan's own international corporate *bengoshi*, who have had a lucrative stream of new foreign clients directed toward them. Had they been willing to permit foreign partnerships, and dared to piggyback for the time being on the American firms' global resources in third-country law, they could have grasped the wide mouth of the cornucopia rather than its narrow tip and integrated themselves as direct and powerful players into the increasingly "borderless" global market for legal services. Overly solicitous for the bird in hand—their own domestic monopoly—and too much the prisoners of their own sociocultural paranoia, Japan's lawyers continue to pass up the greater chance. As a result, Tokyo has denied itself that dynamic mix of a small resident community of foreign lawyers interacting with the domestic legal profession that has turned cities like Paris, London, Brussels, Hong Kong, and Geneva into thriving international legal centers.

Evidence that the incoming foreign lawyers have had any impact at all on Japanese lawyering, let alone on Japanese society, is thus far nil. It is hard to see how the additional step of allowing genuine partnerships—although perhaps stiffening the competition for some marginally energetic Japanese law offices—would seriously dent the established legal and social values, especially in areas other than that of international corporate law, where Japan's 700-some specialists, like international attorneys everywhere, are already imbued with the more aggressive, profit-oriented imperatives of that field.

There is no doubt that most Japanese—as well as increasing numbers of Americans—are repelled by the litigious excesses of late twentieth-century American society, and that they now take it on faith that they are a conciliation-oriented people. It is also true, however, that Japanese plaintiffs have been *forced* toward arbitration and conciliation by the artificial barriers to fuller use of the courts (such as the numerical cap on lawyers and the dilatory scheduling of individual cases), and that some observers in both countries see a lowering of those barriers—meaning more lawyers and litigation—as essential to the health of Japanese democracy and the fuller protection of individual rights. Either way, the culturalist arguments are too macroscopic for calculating the actual impact of such a minuscule number of *gaiben*.

Foreign lawyers stress that they have not come to Japan for ambulance chasing, and they bridle at the insinuation that Japanese lawyers protect human rights whereas Yanks and Brits simply grub for money. They point out that Japan's *pro bono publico* tradition lags well behind that of the U.S., where Japanese lawyers still go to study it. These attorneys and other Japanese sympathetic to the foreigners' position are, unfortunately, reluctant to speak up at the various study committees formed to deliberate the *gaiben* issue. Worse yet, no *gaiben* have ever been allowed to join these committees set up to determine their professional fate in Japan.[17]

Indeed—if I may be permitted to interject my own experience here—Japan does have its own *pro bono publico* lawyers, although they are in a noble minority. One Tokyo firm in 1992 charged me only one-sixth of their normal fee (about $500 instead of $3,000) for many hours of preliminary consultation and research, once they had judged my case to be one of "human rights," involving the private university at which I had been teaching. My application for a renewal of contract had fallen victim to intra-Japanese factional politics after eight months of inconclusive deliberation by my colleagues, the great majority of whom had urged me to reapply. It being much too late in the academic year to find a new job, I decided to sue. We finally settled out of court for a year's salary plus my lawyers' fee (the normal cut of 15 percent of the total sum), but not before the two attorneys on my case had opened my eyes to the powerful corporate and establishmentarian tilt of most of Japan's legal profession.

One day, as we were refining our case, I remarked how odd it seemed that, in the faculty meetings where the matter had come up for discussion (we were a Faculty of Law comprising a Law Department and a Politics Department to which I belonged), none of the law specialists save for one left-wing labor-law authority had ever used terms like "rights," "justice," "fairness," "reciprocity," or "principle" in discussing my eleventh-hour dismissal. My lawyers leaned back to guffaw: "Hall-san, the only legal scholars and practicing attorneys in Japan who use terms like that have all been driven off to the left, into the arms of the socialist and communist parties, labor unions, and consumer groups!" *Driven* was the key word. The big money and prestige attendant on serving the bastions of power and social control were not to be found in fighting for the little man. Hardly a situation unique to Japan, but that's precisely the point: that Japan's system is no more antiseptically idealistic than anyone else's.

The true import of the Japanese cultural argument, as some of the foreign lawyers view it, lies at a deeper level and is more disturbing. Article 27 of the Lawyers Law of 1949 prohibits *bengoshi* from having any continuing professional relationship with any person who is not an "equal legal professional," a category that the JFBA has narrowly interpreted to mean only fellow *bengoshi*. This rules out foreign lawyers, despite their being fully licensed in their home jurisdictions, and the fact that they are required to become special members of the JFBA—a tacit recognition that they are, indeed, fellow "lawyers." Robert Grondine got to the heart of the Americans' frustration with Japan's culturalist pleading when he noted in 1993 that the prohibition on

    . . . partnership and employment relationships seems to be justified solely on the basis that bengoshi and foreign lawyers somehow are different species and therefore cannot work together and should not be allowed to commingle. In my view that policy has led to Nichibenren [the JFBA] justifying its position based upon emotional and cultural arguments which not only have no basis but make it virtually impossible to engage in an objective professional dialogue as to the best interests of society.

Probing for root causes, Grondine suggested a year later that:

. . . the campaign against free relationships with foreign lawyers has its roots in the wider context of a deep-seated tradition of xeno-phobia in Japan, a fear of cultural contamination reflected, in this case, by a need to protect the pure blood of the Japanese legal pro-fession against defilement by mixture with the foreign *barbarians* of old. . . . To those of us who consider ourselves committed interna-tionalists, the continued existence of a Japanese policy of isolating foreign lawyers, especially in what is supposed to be an enlightened profession, is simply abhorrent.[18]

This is pretty strong stuff, coming from the spokesman on this issue for the American Bar Association and the American Chamber of Commerce in Japan.

Japan's own international lawyers, many of them with some training or experience abroad, are a sub-cadre of that echelon in Japan's intellectual elite whose mission for over a hundred years has been to mediate Western ideas and practices for the rest of their countrymen. Their touchiness about their status is in many ways a reaction to the popular view of that bridging function as being somewhat alien and "un-Japanese," and to the disdain in which they are held by Japan's self-defined "true elite," the higher bureaucracy. From the Meiji-period novelist Soseki Natsume—who upon returning from London in 1903 promptly bounced the author Lafcadio Hearn from most of his Tokyo University lecture courses—to some of today's *bengoshi*, there has always been among Japan's acknowledged experts on the West a certain defensiveness toward real flesh-and-blood Westerners who threaten to enter the Japanese system. The single most striking difference between the two systems is, indeed, that in America we don't find the entire U.S. legal profession massively engaged in trying to keep non-Americans out.

The technical objections to opening Japan's legal market are more susceptible to factual argumentation than the woolly cultural premises. Here, the Japanese simply make the most—as Americans typically make the least—of the obvious incongruities between the two respective legal systems, preferring to elevate them into permanent, insurmountable barriers rather than searching for creative accommodations.

The Japanese bar argues that there is no impediment to American lawyers sitting for the LRTI entrance examination beyond their own lack of preparation in Japanese law and language, and the requisite stamina. The assumption here is that the LRTI is Japan's equivalent of a U.S. law school plus bar exam and, as such, an institution for which American lawyers in Japan should also be willing to qualify. The American counterargument is that Japan's severe numerical restriction on its own lawyers *ipso facto* rules out any meaningful reciprocal access, inasmuch as the cut-off points on U.S. state bar exams are purely qualitative, with the size of the American lawyer pool determined by market forces alone.

The LRTI pass line—set by government policy at 500 in 1963 and tiptoeing toward 1,000 by the end of this century—has never taken into account the number or abilities of Japanese wishing to take the test in any given year. Japan's deliberate rationing of legal professionals not only serves the purpose of social control by discouraging litigation; as the Tokyo-based economic journalist Eamonn Fingleton has pointed out, Japanese authorities view it also as supporting the nation's growth-oriented industrial policy by putting a lid on one of the less productive service industries—although University of Chicago scholar J. Mark Ramseyer has argued that in fact there are broad economic losses from a legal profession that spends so much of its energies maintaining a cartel that serves partly to transfer, rather than create, wealth.[19] Douglas Kenji Freeman, the one American who *has* passed through the LRTI, has often been cited by the Japanese bar as proof that foreigners can make it into the system. Freeman, who passed the test in

1993 at the age of 26, reportedly played down his accomplishment to the press, however, explaining that he has a Japanese mother and has always lived in Japan.[20]

The JFBA further claims that the U.S. legal system is actually less open and generous to foreign lawyers than is Japan's, on three counts. Foreigners are allowed to practice in Japan without having passed the "Japanese bar exam" at the LRTI; Japanese (like American) lawyers who pass a bar exam in the U.S. are qualified to practice only in that one state; and most U.S. states do not permit Japanese who have not qualified in the U.S. to practice at all. The third complaint simply misinterprets the absence of rules for Foreign Legal Consultants in many U.S. states as an active intent to debar them, and 22 American jurisdictions now follow New York's 1974 rules covering FLCs who have not qualified locally and are restricted to advising on their home country law—the precise reciprocal, in other words, of the American *gaiben* in Japan. This category, however, is a minuscule sideshow for foreign lawyers in the U.S., and the other two complaints—about examinations and jurisdictions—overlook the vastly greater freedom of access and operation for non-Americans within the U.S. mainstream of the profession.

It is the crucial difference in *opportunity* for admission to the other country's legal mainstream that is most responsible for the imbalance between Japan and America in the legal services field. The primary route whereby Japanese *bengoshi* obtain access to the American legal system is by becoming fully admitted as a lawyer upon passing the bar exam in one of the American states. This is a status that can be maintained indefinitely wherever they may be working since it does not include the residency requirement incumbent on foreign lawyers in Japan. As of 1996 over 150 *bengoshi*—a number that continues to climb rapidly—have taken this route into the U.S. mainstream, where they enjoy the "full run" of the system with exactly the same rights and privileges as American attorneys. Most of them are members of the major Japanese international law firms in Tokyo; some have become partners in major American law firms. They are free to work for either Japanese or American law firms and corporations in the U.S., advising on Japanese law while practicing American. By contrast, only four

Japanese have bothered to register in the U.S. as "foreign legal consultants" without taking an American bar exam.

Out of a 1993 U.S.-wide total of 111 *bengoshi* who had passed the bar exam, more than 86 had done so in New York, and 14 in California, the next most popular location. It is from these hubs of overseas commerce and international law practice in the U.S. that Japanese *bengoshi*, like their American colleagues, maintain and service clients nationwide. Parallel geographical concentrations obtain for the headquartering of Japanese corporations in the U.S., and for the FLCs of all nationalities registered in the 22 American jurisdictions that have adopted specific systems for them. These states—all key ones for international business—include New York, New Jersey, Connecticut, California, Oregon, Washington, Hawaii, Illinois, Michigan, Ohio, Texas, and the District of Columbia. There is neither need nor demand for Japanese *bengoshi* to open offices in Vermont or Wyoming, and the JFBA complaints about states without FLC systems—like the hypothetical need to pass 50 bar exams to match Japan's unitary national jurisdiction—are no more than rhetorical red herrings.[21]

Meanwhile, in Japan, the fundamental unfairness lies in a system that permits Japanese law offices to employ foreign lawyers but not vice versa, and allows *bengoshi* qualified in the law of both countries to practice both as long as they are in the U.S., yet forces those who return to Japan with a foreign firm (like Mr. Terai) to suspend their *bengoshi* status and qualification to practice Japanese law while back in Japan. American lawyers view Japan's restricting of law practice to LRTI-qualified *bengoshi* as "a narrow interpretation of Article VIII of the U.S.-Japan Treaty of Friendship and Commerce which under one reading could be interpreted as allowing professionals of both countries to practice in either."[22] Since Japan's international lawyers are neither sufficiently numerous nor networked abroad to service Japan's global legal needs by themselves, this dog-in-the-manger protection of a small interest group comes at the expense of both countries' greater economic interests.

American observers have noted both the economic and political losses incurred by the U.S. thanks to this lawyer imbalance. As the political scholar on Japan, Chalmers

Johnson, has noted, the refusal to allow American *gaiben* to hire or to enter into partnerships with Japanese *bengoshi* "essentially renders American firms defenseless in the face of the Japanese legal system." He contrasts this with the full run that corporate Japan has enjoyed of America's open opportunities for lobbying and litigation, citing Toshiba's hiring of the New York firm of Mudge, Rose, Guthrie, Alexander & Ferndon to defend itself against threatened U.S. sanctions for illegally selling top-secret machinery to the former USSR, and Matsushita's engagement of former U.S. trade representative Robert Strauss to help the political expediting of its purchase of Universal Studios. "No American firm," Johnson rightly concludes, "could possibly obtain the same legal services in Japan."[23] The skewed legal field affects U.S diplomatic leverage as well. Referring to what an American trade negotiator called "really an intolerable imbalance," an American journalist reported that:

> U.S. legal experts have complained for years that the small presence American lawyers have in Japan puts U.S. business and government officials at a disadvantage when it comes to negotiating terms of contracts or trade agreements. In short, these experts contend, Americans don't understand Japan's legal system as well as Japanese understand the U.S. system, and the lack of American lawyers in Japan is an important reason for the disparity.[24]

THE CAST OF CHARACTERS

The legal services dispute has followed a pattern that holds for the door-opening campaigns of the other professions as well. Fitful foreign pressures for access finally muster enough focus to force some attention to the issue by Japan. Amid distracting public-relations hoopla about Japan at last changing and opening up, Tokyo draws up new regulations and systems—more explicit and detailed than anything previous—that are intended to make minimal concessions and lock them into a permanent new order that will be proof against any real opening. Initially euphoric about the new dispensation, the foreign postulants eventually realize they have bought a pig in a

poke; but by then both they and the governments who supported them have reverted to their chronic lack of institutional
memory and organizational staying power, too tired to gird up
for yet another round.

In conclusion, a word about the minor players in the legal
services dispute, voices that will be recognized later in the other
professional sectors. Japanese support for the foreign lawyers
has been most pronounced among the business community, its
governmental allies, and its leading media tribune, the *Nihon
Keizai Shinbun* (Japan Economic Journal). The U.S. push for
complete liberalization of commercial arbitration procedures,
for example—including the right of foreign counsel to represent
clients in Japanese arbitrations—was all along enthusiastically
backed, in the interest of expedited trade, by the influential Keidanren, the Ministry of International Trade and Industry
(MITI), and the Japan Commercial Arbitration Association.
Meanwhile, the JFBA and the Ministry of Justice drew out a
resolution of the issue with yet another study group to which,
once again, no non-Japanese were invited.

A Keidanren report in October 1992 calling for the liberalization of legal services described the existing situation as
"unnatural."[25] "Japan's systems and rules need to be reformed
into ones more harmonious with the international community,
and legal services cannot be allowed to remain a sacred cow,"
intoned an advisory body to the Office of Trade Ombudsman
during the negotiations of 1993, worried—as was the Foreign
Ministry—about Japan's image abroad as the torrent of foreign
complaints poured in.[26] Arguing in an editorial that the official
social-service ideal of Japan's profession was not at odds with
the quest for improved services and that, "easing rules on
foreign lawyers will unclog Japan's legal logjam," the *Nihon
Keizai Shinbun* in 1993 urged Japan to "play a pioneering role
in market liberalization."[27] Susumu Hirano, at the time a corporate counsel at Fuji Heavy Industries, Ltd.'s legal department,
argued in 1993 that, "The shortage of lawyers alone indicates
significant opportunities for foreign lawyers to practice in
Japan."[28] A December 1990 poll conducted by the Association
of Japanese Corporate Legal Departments revealed 43 percent
of respondents in favor of lifting the rules limiting foreign

lawyers, while only 26 percent found the existing restrictions acceptable. Among those most likely to benefit are the smaller companies, which find it difficult to find the right overseas law firm.[29]

There is no doubt that these expressions of economic and political good sense by the forward-looking elements in Japanese business, government, and press circles and among the *bengoshi* themselves are sincerely meant. Unfortunately, as in the other areas we shall look at, public pressures that move the issue along in a Western society run up against that wall of semi-impermeable autonomy that has characterized so many of the subgroups of Japanese society in the postwar period. The tendency of Japanese to defer to each vested interest in questions affecting its own turf—meaning, in the case of lawyers, the stand-pat and xenophobic forces that dominate the JFBA—has set a pattern for Japan's internationalist elements, always a minority, backing down in the end.

The oddest counterpoint to Japan's liberalizing voices are those foreign apologists who belittle the need for liberalization in the first instance and then, when a small breakthrough has been achieved, decry the attempt at further progress. As has often been noted with respect to the U.S. business community in Japan, there have also been American lawyers—among the old Occupation-period holdovers, and some of those first through the door under the new law of 1986—who are ready to echo the Japanese line that the market is not really all that closed, or, if it is, that it really doesn't matter that much. Indeed, some of the larger East and West Coast firms that pioneered the new openings of 1986 were content to live with the lucrative new business they were doing with Japanese corporations entering the U.S. market and to leave to another day the task of creating wider opportunities in Japan for all American lawyers. Joining the Japanese after both the new law in 1986 and the amendments of 1994 in calling for a "testing period" of several years, they distanced themselves from what they dubbed the "radical" contingent among American lawyers in Tokyo. These so-called radicals are mostly younger attorneys with considerable Japanese experience who see themselves as trade facilitators for American companies seeking to enter the Japanese market and who are, therefore, committed to full legal access, no matter how long or difficult the goal.[30]

In 1987, with the new law just come into effect, E. Anthony Zaloom of the New York firm Skadden, Arps, Slate, Meagher & Flom, skirted the issue of hiring or partnering with Japanese lawyers. He also brushed off the admittedly "many restrictions in the new law" as being of little practical consequence:

> None of them, however, is a serious obstacle to successfully practicing law here. A gaikokuho jimu bengoshi is not allowed to appear in court, but hardly any of us coming here are litigators. Rather, we are so-called business lawyers, whose job it is to help plan business transactions and negotiate and draft contracts. A gaikokuho jimu bengoshi is not allowed to practice Japanese law, but most of us know little or nothing about Japanese law anyway.[31]

European law firms have injected a wavering, third-country voice into the noisy U.S.-Japan dissonance while normally sitting with the American choir. With little support from their own governments, which lack any significant leverage on Japan, they are happy to reap the benefits of official U.S. pressures on Tokyo—a pattern that has been repeated with foreign journalists and professors. British firms, which comprise most of the third-country presence, come with a demonstrated commitment to Asia honed at former imperial outposts like Singapore and Hong Kong. They are in fact better prepared than the Americans to meet Tokyo's high costs by imposing stiff-upper-lip ceilings on salaries and office space.

Japan's lawyers can hardly be faulted for trying to drive a wedge between the Americans and Europeans, in two ways. One has been to harp on the differences between the U.S. and Continental legal traditions, the similarities between Japanese and European practices, and the intra-European barriers to foreign lawyers that the EU itself is seeking to remove, asking why the U.S. should single out Japan for such extraordinary attention. The JFBA pointed out that *étatiste* France (a perennial favorite with Japan's apologists, as we shall see with the universities) permitted only those foreign lawyers to form partnerships who had passed the French bar exam and registered as an *avocat*. That parallel crumbled when France integrated its *avocats* (lawyers) and *conseils juridiques* (legal advisors) in a single profession in 1992, whereupon Japan suspended its "reciprocity" for French lawyers.

JFBA representatives also took advantage of the divergence in European and American priorities at a private tripartite conference in Evian, France, in October 1993, just before the wrapup of GATT negotiations in Geneva that December. The Europeans were themselves divided over foreign lawyer access as between their own countries, and, because of their lengthier pre-practice apprenticeship periods, were more interested in shortening the five-year home-country practice requirement than in supporting the American push for Japan-foreign partnerships. Moving deftly into the gap, the Japanese delegation managed to line up the Europeans behind their "joint enterprise" proposal, a result that was widely criticized by European lawyers practicing in Japan. That plan, designed to prevent genuine partnerships, was then promptly endorsed by the GATT negotiators and enshrined in Japan's amended rules for foreign lawyers in 1994.[32]

Finally, the failure of the West to unite in efforts to pry open the Japanese door now makes it the more likely that Japan's closed system, thus ratified, will spread to its Asian neighbors. Indeed, the visit of a Korean delegation in 1994 to study Japan's arrangements for foreign lawyers augurs that Tokyo's success in getting American attorneys to settle for so little may eventually make Japanese-style barriers and the arguments in favor of them the accepted pattern in East Asia, thereby pegging the whole region at a low level of mutual access and of minimal openness to the West. The formula: allow half the foreign foot inside the gate, then lock it firmly against the aching arches.

2

SEGREGATED SCRIBES
The Foreign Correspondents

On 21 May 1993, the Asian bureau chief of Bloomberg Business News and a fellow American reporter "stormed" the Kabuto Club at the Tokyo Stock Exchange, entering the premises of one of Japan's exclusive reporters' clubs (*kisha kurabu*) to demand immediate access to market-moving earnings reports as they were being distributed to Japanese newsmen on the busiest day of the corporate earnings season. For today's computerized financial news services, even one minute's lag in coming on-line can render one's statistics stale in the global competition. After two years of fruitless negotiation for membership in the Kabuto Club, David Butts was there to protest the delay—anywhere from five to fifteen minutes—in receiving the financial reports as he and other foreign correspondents waited outside in the hallway with their portable phones, at desks and in-boxes provided by the club.

From the time this tall 36-year-old Texan was still in his cradle, the foreign press in Tokyo had been fighting for access to the news sources monopolized by the "kisha clubs" attached to each of Japan's government ministries, to major corporations, business federations, labor unions, prominent politicians, political parties, and party factions, and to leading social and cultural institutions. Not even the press's umbrella organization, the Nihon Shinbun

Kyokai (NSK: the Japan Newspaper Publishers and Editors Association) knows the actual number of these clubs. Estimates can be found ranging from the 440 identified in 1993 by the semi-governmental Foreign Press Center to perhaps as many as 1,000, including local branches, throughout the country.[1]

After a 45-minute standoff during which he and his colleague were physically stopped from receiving the press releases, Butts left, accusing the stock exchange's club of "discrimination"—to which Japanese newsmen retorted that he had sowed "confusion" by not keeping to his alloted station.[2] Most adamantly opposed to Bloomberg's admission was the *Nihon Keizai Shinbun*, Japan's equivalent of the *Wall Street Journal* and forty percent owner of a Japanese financial news service whose box at the Kabuto Club was always the first to receive company announcements. Three days later Butts repeated his intrusion, vowing to settle for nothing less than a desk, telephone, and pigeonhole next to his Japanese competitors, inside the door.

Bucking the received wisdom that one should never go against Japanese etiquette or sensitivities, Butts was gambling that some aggressive, negative publicity could only help. He was right. Before long, the American Embassy—as with lawyers, there was a trade angle and big money involved here—swung behind the 35-year effort to open Japan's kisha club system to foreign correspondents. By year's end AP-Dow Jones, Britain's Reuters, and Bloomberg were all inside the Kabuto Club door. Tokyo was witnessing another one of those grudging and minimalist— though, as always, hopefully heralded—openings to non-Japanese professionals whereby a few more foreign journalists find themselves permitted to participate in the activities of a few more of Japan's hundreds of reporters' clubs.

Far more was at stake, however, than the split-second corporate advantages featured in this confrontation. In interviews with the press over the months of his campaign, Butts consistently put his finger on the true root and significance of the problem:

> The Japanese media have a cartel which they use to control information, and they don't want any cracks to emerge in that cartel. . . .

They are also concerned that foreign reporters may write from a different perspective. They want to keep it cushy and comfy.[3]

They're journalists organizing together to exclude other journalists. . . . That's repugnant, disgusting.[4] There's more danger inherent in trying to control or limit the press than there is in assuring that it's free. . . . It was something we had to do, it was an obligation to the most important principles of journalism: free and open access to information and free distribution of that information. . . . What we faced in Japan was suppression of the press, not by the government, but by other members of the press, which we thought was just egregious.[5]

Seven years earlier, in 1986, BBC bureau chief William Horsley had noted the essential character of the kisha clubs:

They are, in effect, cartels, fixing the distribution—and often the value—of the information they glean.[6]

Of Japan's various cartels of the mind, the one in journalism is indeed "egregious." It is the intellectual cartel most obvious to the eye; the one most deeply set in the formal structures and working habits of an entire profession; the one with the most baneful impact on the exchange of ideas with other countries; the one most restrictive of an open and democratic flow of information among the Japanese themselves; and the only such cartel actually threatened with collapse should outsiders really be allowed to participate. The kisha club system also represents the Japanese intellectual barrier longest under assault by organized foreign professionals seeking access—ever since 1960, with only marginal results. As such, it richly illustrates not only Japan's consummate skills at procrastination, evasion, and the psychological stringing along of would-be intruders—as more recently witnessed in trade talks—but also those foreign foibles for distraction, lack of institutional memory, and wishful thinking, which play so readily into Japanese hands.

Nothing more dramatically exposes Japan's recalcitrance—its determination *not* to dismantle *any* of its cartels of the mind— than the seemingly intractable confrontation between the kisha clubs and the NSK on the one hand and the two representative organizations of the resident foreign press on the other. These are the Foreign Correspondents' Club of Japan (FCCJ)—the professional and social association for most of Tokyo's 400-some accredited foreign journalists, dating from 1945, which hosts luncheon speakers and press conferences and provides library, workroom, and dining facilities for its members—and the Foreign Press in Japan (FPIJ), an affiliated organization based on company rather than individual memberships that was set up in 1960 to negotiate with the Japanese for space allocations at major news events and to push for access to the kisha club system.

First, then, the broader context of the kisha club problem, followed by a ringside-seat view of this decades-long skirmish between Japanese and foreign journalists.

A HI-TECH FEUDAL PRESS

Like the legal system, the manner of gathering and disseminating news in Japan differs substantially from that practiced elsewhere. One of the greatest anomalies of the Japanese press is its blending of one of the world's most technically advanced, elaborately organized, and intellectually sophisticated mass media systems with a feudal crazyquilt of protectionist kisha club guilds that routinely violate at least three of the basic canons of modern journalism in a free society. The cozy, collusive ties between sources and club reporters discourage an aggressive, let alone adversarial, pursuit of the truth, turning the journalist all too often into a conduit for the source's spin on the news. The collaboration (and mutual monitoring) among the club members themselves contributes to that virtual identity of layout and that bland, noncontroversial conformity of reportage and interpretation so often noted among Japan's competing news organizations. And the notion of the public's right to know—including that of the international public—has simply been ignored by the clubs, sources, and NSK alike.

On the modern side, Japan's mass media are massive in scale, financially secure, staffed by graduates of the nation's most prestigious universities, furnished with every conceivable hi-tech gimmick, yet lavishly labor-intensive with armies of reporters and photographers on any major story, including the largest number of correspondents from any single country stationed abroad—638 of them on six continents as of 1995, with 181 in the U.S. alone. They cater to one of the world's largest, most literate, and news-hungry national readerships and TV audiences. Japan's five great national dailies (*Yomiuri, Asahi, Mainichi, Nihon Keizai,* and *Sankei*) all publish separate morning and evening papers and in 1995 boasted circulations (for the morning papers alone) of 10.1, 8.3, 4.0, 2.9, and 1.9 million respectively—weekday figures that tower over the *New York Times'* 1.1 million or the 1.8 million for America's largest paper, the *Wall Street Journal.* Unlike the regional radius of major U.S. dailies, Japan's great newspapers face off in direct and ferocious competition in a single nationwide market, yet they have opted to gain and maintain their edge not by being different but by sticking closely to what their rivals are covering and opining.

Pride of place in Japanese television is held by a gargantuan semiautonomous public entity, the Japan Broadcasting Corporation (NHK: the Nippon Hoso Kyokai), which toes the government's line more faithfully than does its British counterpart and model, the BBC. Unlike British television, however, Japan has for decades had a robust commercial sector providing serious programming together with variety and spunk to offset the often schoolmarmish staidness of NHK. The five national commercial networks, however, are owned by and reflect the respective editorial outlook of the five national dailies—thereby adding a warp of vertical integration to the cartelizing woof of the kisha clubs and further helping to homogenize Japan's news business.

These papers and networks, known as the "elite press," dominate the kisha club system, although there often are separate clubs for the print and electronic media, with television further divided between NHK and the private-sector broadcasters collectively known as Minpo. Also in the system are the four large region-wide "block" dailies published at Sapporo, Nagoya, Hiroshima, and Fukuoka, and Japan's two wire services, Kyodo Tsushin and Jiji Tsushin. Where there are multiple clubs attached to a source, the national dailies, NHK, and the larger Kyodo Tsushin are typically in the top drawer, with the regional dailies, Minpo, and the Jiji wire service relegated to the second tier.

Below these privileged castes come the pariahs routinely excluded from the reporters' clubs: the racy weeklies, the ponderous opinion monthlies, the whole gamut of specialized publications, all freelancers no matter how well-known and influential, and the foreign correspondents—who find themselves, actually, in pretty good company if one likes a more aggressive, investigative type of journalism than that filtered through the kisha club sieve by Japan's prestige press.

Since Japan's national dailies already convey the sort of comprehensive coverage of domestic and overseas events supplied in America's geographically fragmented newspaper market by *Time, Newsweek*, and *U.S. News & World Report*, Japanese weekly magazines limit themselves to a lighter potpourri of political gossip, social scandal, and serialized fiction. In a further extension of vertical cartelization, roughly half of the weeklies are also owned by the five national dailies. However, the very fact that they are not to be taken too "seriously" enables them to raise questions, drop hints, and utter plain truths that would be taboo for the elite press. Such items are tolerated in the weeklies since they can be easily discounted as the babblings of lowbrow journalism.

At the opposite pole of sophistication, Japan's dozen bulky intellectual monthlies offer two to three hundred pages apiece of essays on current issues by scholars, officials, business people, and assorted literati. Although lacking the literary elegance of America's two general-purpose monthlies, the *Atlantic* and *Harper's*, they present a wide and immediately accessible national forum of ideas that in the U.S. would have to be culled from a long list of more narrowly-guaged journals like *Foreign Affairs, Daedalus*, or the *National Review*. It is in the monthlies, too, that Japan's hardy band of corporately unemployable investigative freelancers most often find their voice. Indeed, the classic triumph of the kisha-club outsiders over the self-censorship of the reporters' clubs came in October 1974, when the foreign press picked up on an exposé of Prime Minister Kakuei Tanaka's irregular acquisition of funds that had been researched and written by one of Tokyo's most aggressive independent journalists, Takashi Tachibana. Tachibana's article was first carried in the monthly *Bungei Shunju*, and only then taken up by the daily press corps. But it was overseas attention that drove the case, and within weeks of his disastrous grilling at an FCCJ press luncheon, Tanaka resigned as prime minister.

Japanese reporters were not always as conformist as they are today. As with many countries in the initial phase of modern development (including the revolutionary-era U.S.), Japanese journalism got its start in the Meiji period (1868–1912) as an outgrowth of political pamphleteering. It provided an outlet for the frustrated energies of samurai intellectuals who had been stripped of their feudal social status and hereditary rice stipends and were out of sympathy with the autocratic Tokyo government. The traits of these original Japanese reporters as brainy, politicized, national-interest-oriented and antiauthoritarian stalwarts can still be found today. Their adversarial antigovernment stance has largely been reduced to a pose, but the old xenophobic political nationalism remains strong. From 1875 onward, however, stringent press-control laws brought this early-stage political journalism sharply to heel, and by the turn of the century Japan, with its burgeoning urban culture centered on the Tokyo and Osaka regions, was well into the business of mass-circulation commercial journalism, in step with the raucous Hearst papers in the U.S. and the great London dailies.

The topsy-turvy conventions of today's Japanese press dictate that newspaper editorials and TV news commentaries be tame and elliptical—while winking at rampant editorializing in headlines, photo captions, and the obiter dicta of TV news documentaries. Newspaper staff roundtables on issues of the day are usually anonymous, with participants merely identified as journalists "A," "B," and "C." Bylines or original news stories by individual correspondents are virtually unknown in the dailies, which—somewhat in the manner of *Time* and *Newsweek*, as it happens—reprocess everything at the editor's desk to fit the house style and normally the house line, too, crediting reporters mainly for the raw information. More than ever before, the typical Japanese journalist today has been driven by his working context to become a cautious *sarariman*, like the millions of fellow white-collared "salarymen" for which he (or, very rarely in a heavily male-dominated profession, she) writes. It is a pity, since, in private, I have found among Japanese newspeople some of the most open-minded, frankly spoken, and gregarious members of Japan's intellectual elite.

It is within this conservatively tilted matrix that the kisha clubs play their problematical, reinforcing, role. Whereas press conferences in other free countries are organized and controlled by the sources and are open to all credentialed journalists, most of the news originating in Japan is filtered through formal, on-the-record press conferences (*kisha kaiken*) and informal, off-the-record background briefings (*kondan*) with individual or institutional sources that are organized by, and restricted to, members of the respective kisha clubs. About half of a given news organization's reportorial staff may be assigned full-time for about two years to specific kisha club beats, with the remaining reporters placed on roving coverage or editing-desk duties. Club members normally spend most of their working hours in spaces provided by their sources—in the case of the government ministries, that means at taxpayers' expense. Here, among a crowded jumble of desks, files, telephones, computers, teapots, and hot-water thermoses, they typically hunker down for the day to read up on developments, await scheduled sessions, and store up energy for their "night ambushes" and "forays at dawn" to the front doorsteps of prominent officials and politicians in hopes of catching them in a more relaxed or unguarded mood as they leave home or return from work.

The first kisha club was established at the insistence of reporters in 1890 at the Diet building to insure news access to Japan's new parliamentary system inaugurated that year. Japanese publishers subsequently backed their individual reporters' efforts to organize clubs as a means of prying information out of the haughty civil and military bureaucracies, while government ministries found it useful to have a unified channel for their own releases. It was during the ideologically turbulent 1920s and 1930s that Japanese journalists came closest to resembling their Western counterparts. There were still "lone wolf" newsmen on the dailies who went after scoops and exclusives on their own initiative and wrote under their own name. In spite of strict press laws, which no longer burden their more timid successors today, the kisha clubs of the interwar era often assumed a confrontational, watchdog posture toward the government, at times even bringing down high officials who got in their way. Still organized "horizontally" as mutual-help associations of individual journalists, they also served a trade-union function in standing up to the news company owners.

All of this changed with mobilization for war. It was not the military censorship from 1937 on that made the lasting difference—Japanese journalists had long dealt with those cruder sorts of pressures—but the structural "reform" of the kisha club system imposed by the government in 1942. In a consolidation reminiscent of those forced on Japan's political parties and religious bodies after 1940, the number of press clubs in Tokyo was reduced from some 100 to only 18. A new organization of publishers, the Nippon Newspaper Association (NNA: also, in Japanese, the Nippon Shinbun Kyokai) was placed under government supervision and given control, in turn, of the kisha clubs; and membership in the clubs themselves was changed from an individual to company basis and restricted to ten news organizations—the then elite press.[7]

This protectionist triangle of establishment sources, media moguls, and elite reporters survived the war and explains the tenacious persistence of the kisha club system today. The government continues to enjoy a powerful spin on the news through its established channels of co-opted journalists; publishers have less to fear from excessively individualistic, ideologically heterodox, or antimanagement reporters; and a privileged coterie of news organizations continues to enjoy its monopolistic lien on the sources.

The routine apologia for the system today is, of course, never put so crudely. Nor does anyone really believe the NSK's frequent pronouncements to the effect that the clubs are primarily social in function and only tangentially engaged in news gathering, because news gathering is precisely what they do. The argument runs, rather, that the clubs provide a way of moving news more efficiently and fairly (than, say, the shouting

matches of the old Carter White House presidential press conferences). It is said that the trust established between sources
and club reporters through ongoing personal contact (together
with the self-policing group ethos of the newsmen themselves)
allows the source to delve more deeply into sensitive matters,
knowing that each club member will respect his needs for circumspection or face expulsion by his own colleagues, and that
the reporters more than make up in long-term collective insight
whatever they might be losing in ego-building exclusives
splashed across tomorrow's front page. And of course the sen-
sationalistic gutter press is kept at bay.

Foreign correspondents are held to be unfit for club participation because they are said to lack the requisite language skills
(true of some but by no means all). It is also argued that foreign
correspondents operate for the most part as one- or two-person
offices, and hence cannot devote the time necessary to fit
smoothly into any single club. And with their free-wheeling,
doggedly probing manner, Western (and other Asian) newspeople cannot be trusted to maintain club confidences. The
most important news normally originates in the relaxed, homey
setting of the *kondan* background sessions, where notebooks
are put away, drinks and banter flow, and the participating
reporters huddle at the finish to decide the spin or self-restraint
on any given story. In short, the clubs' delicately stacked china
would be knocked to pieces by the participation of untamed
foreign bulls.

Occasionally Japanese reporters and sources will admit that
they simply do not feel comfortable with foreigners, but the
facts that more foreigners now do have a functional fluency in
Japanese, or that they have Japanese staff they could send in
their stead, or that the clubs themselves always have a certain
number of Japanese members with multiple club beats who are
there only part-time, are conveniently overlooked. Most
important, in thinking up all the possible reasons for systematically excluding foreign journalists in Japan, the clubs resolutely
ignore the fundamental issue of reciprocity: Japanese correspondents in Western capitals are limited only by their shoe
leather and command of the local language—not by any social
discomfort the local journalists might feel in their presence, nor

by any barriers to doing their job that have been raised against them merely because they are Japanese.

THE HAPPY-GO-LUCKY YEARS

It was on this clubby door that Tokyo's foreign correspondents began knocking from around 1960, launching the second of three phases that were to define their postwar relation to Japan's kisha club system. First came the years of lofty indifference toward the Japanese news industry, from MacArthur's landing in 1945 to Crown Prince Akihito's wedding in 1958. From 1960 to 1985 came a quarter century of intermittent begging for favors rewarded by a placative scrap or two. Finally, in the past decade (1985–1995), there has been a tougher and more sustained push, demanding guaranteed access to on-the-record events or even full membership in the clubs themselves—so far with only modest and still indeterminate results.

The Foreign Correspondents' Club of Japan was founded by the American journalists who first came in with MacArthur's army of occupation. They had long endured the taunts of the Supreme Commander's public relations chief, Brigadier General Legrange Diller, who derided them during the Pacific campaign as a bunch of "two bit palookas and sports writers." "Killer" Diller immediately sought to impose strict quotas on the influx of foreign reporters—Britain was to get only four—pleading a shortage of suitable billets. The Americans, many of them seasoned war correspondents who had lost colleagues on the battlefield, objected on principle and quickly established their own press association open to any incoming reporter "whatever his creed, race, or color." In the fall of 1945 they were duly assisted by occupation headquarters in securing and refurbishing their own hostel in a five-story, run-down Japanese restaurant building. Food, liquor, blankets, and phonograph records poured in *gratis* from U.S. forces and the Red Cross, as indigent Japanese college students, service workers, and self-styled "geishas" queued up—2,000 of them on the first day—for the 70 jobs available. Before long, the FCCJ was boasting the best food, drink, and social program in town. With poetic justice, thirsty majors and colonels were turned away at the door unless accompanied by a "two-bit palooka."[8]

This was a heady start, high above the flattened rubble of Tokyo, and a convenient oasis and base-camp for forays into the successive trouble-spots of continental Asia. For over a decade, American journalists were focused less on the subtleties of the Japan scene than on the Big Picture—on the achievements and foibles of the Occupation and the more dramatic events in China and Korea as war correspondents from Asian battlefronts flew into Tokyo to file their stories, grab a decent meal, and spread their sleeping bags in the lobby of the FCCJ. Since Japan had no national press club of its own until 1969 (and no building until 1976), it became a ritual for visiting world figures—be they Prime Minister Nehru, Princess Margaret, or Muhammad Ali—to deliver a luncheon address at the FCCJ. In an era when Japan's own party politics came across as inconsequential and opaque, global newsmakers—if not the internal politicking of the FCCJ itself—often seemed the more challenging beat. Much of the direct news gathering during these years was performed by the bilingual Americans of Japanese ancestry who had come over with the Occupation, while deeper probing below the surface of Japanese political and social change was left to those who had the time to write books—to freelancers, novelists, or the budding corps of academic Japanologists. In short, no one during the early postwar period could have cared less about access to Japan's kisha clubs.

By the late 1950s, however, Japan was back on its feet with its own equivalent of West Germany's better-known *Wirtschafts-wunder*, or "economic miracle," and was once again attracting international news attention in its own right. A series of front-page events around the turn of decade—including Crown Prince Akihito's wedding in 1958 and the massive riots protesting the new security treaty and President Eisenhower's planned visit in 1960—led to the establishment that year of the FCCJ-affiliated Foreign Press in Japan. One purpose was to present a unified front among competing foreign news organizations in negotiations for seats and camera positions at front-page news events; another was to seek access to some of the kisha clubs' regular on-the-record activities. By 1965 there were 130 foreign correspondents in Tokyo hailing from 16 different countries. Yet in

1964, when U.S. Ambassador Edwin Reischauer was stabbed in an assassination attempt, not even the American correspondents could attend the press conference at the nearby police station that had arrested the assailant, because they were not members of the press club attached to the metropolitan police. And when the Japanese press club covering the U.S. embassy claimed exclusive rights to the story, American journalists could do nothing but howl.

With such anomalies abounding, the successive presidents of the FCCJ launched a yearly litany of pleas in their customary greetings at the annual conventions of the NSK. Starting in October of 1965, John Roderick of the Associated Press made it clear that the foreign press was being critical not of the kisha clubs as such but of their membership policy, and appealed for access only to formal on-the-record press conferences (*kisha kaiken*), not to the more cozy *kondan* or to membership in the clubs themselves. If the clubs refused, he requested that the Japanese government hold its own separate conferences for foreign reporters. It all fell on deaf ears, because three years later Henry Hartzenbusch (also AP) spoke more pointedly to the NSK as he noted Japan's spectacular economic growth and the surge of interest in economic news from Tokyo. But, he complained:

> . . . it seems contradictory that news coverage of Japan by foreign correspondents continues to be impeded by a handful of so-called reporters' clubs, and it seems disappointing that the newspaper publishers and editors of some of the world's largest newspapers seem helpless in this situation. News is not a commodity to be consciously exported. It is a commodity that exports itself.[9]

The attitude of the foreign press toward its Japanese counterpart wove uncertainly between barely bridled anger and culturally relativist conciliation, as when Italian FCCJ head Ugo Puntieri (ANSA), while addressing the same shopworn pleas to the NSK in 1969, grandly allowed that:

> . . . we foreign correspondents are not here at all to teach you how to run your shop. . . . Our readers are totally different and so are our

professional interests, our angles, our requirements and our ethical codes of conduct. Basic differences that are making both of us no competitor at all to the other. . . . [10]

But Puntieri's warning that foreign journalists frustrated in their search for information might file angry and exaggerated stories on Japan may have had some effect as cracks began to appear in the system early in the new decade. While noting these with effusive optimism for the future, FCCJ president Mack Chrysler (*U.S. News & World Report*) nevertheless had some harsh words for the kisha club system at the 1972 convention of the NSK:

The parochial approach to news coverage may have been tolerable in past years when Japan was a tight little island nation with relatively little impact on international affairs. It no longer is today when Japanese views and Japanese actions are of paramount importance to policy-makers and people in other countries of the world. [11]

The standpattism of the Japanese press during these years was clear from a letter addressed by the NSK to the International Press Institute in Zurich in response to foreign complaints, and in a put-down of those complaints in the NSK's own weekly organ, both in the fall of 1968. Referring to the usual "peculiarities" of the kisha clubs that were "not fully understood" by foreign correspondents, the letter to the IPI resurrected the old myth that the clubs were mere social groupings that had somehow been backed willy-nilly into professional reportorial structures for which the sources, rather than the clubs themselves, were responsible—and that they had no intention, of course, of monopolizing the news. The Houdini-like casuistic contortions delivered here with a totally straight face are worth quoting at length since they epitomize the amorphous Japanese "logic" that the foreign press has had to contend with over the past quarter century:

The peculiarity of Japanese reporters' clubs lies in the fact that they are not only organs for fostering friendship among members but at the same time are organs having news-gathering functions. Because reporters' clubs have their premises within the offices of the various ministries of the government and the headquarters of various political parties, and because they are composed of reporters who are assigned over long periods of time exclusively to specific news sources, the reporters' clubs *cannot avoid engaging* in news-gathering activities. . . .

However, reporters' clubs are, first and foremost, organs of mutual friendship. If this characteristic of reporters' clubs is taken into consideration, it goes without saying that *they cannot hinder the news-gathering activities of press representatives who do not belong to the clubs, neither can they monopolize news sources. As a matter of fact, there are no cases of reporters' clubs consciously engaged in monopolizing news sources.* However, some news sources welcome the news-gathering activities of reporters with whom they are in constant contact and tend to dislike news-gathering by reporters other than members of reporters' clubs. . . .

The criticism that "reporters' clubs monopolize news sources" we believe arises from this fact. However, the *responsibility for this situation does not lie with the reporters' clubs but with the news source* [emphasis added throughout].[12]

Here is the triangle of evasion that foreign correspondents still chase around: Japan's umbrella press organization, the NSK, denies any influence over the kisha clubs, citing their voluntary and autonomous character; the clubs in turn blame the problem on their sources; and any source that a foreign newsperson appeals to is likely to refer the supplicant back to the NSK. The NSK's in-house newsletter, *Shinbun Kyokaiho*, of 15 October 1968, firmly rejected the foreign grievances in a survey of the kisha clubs. Noting that U.S. presidents from time to time meet privately with an inner circle of American reporters, the NSK still failed to see—or chose to ignore—the essential distinction between on-the-record conferences to which the FCCJ and FPIJ were seeking admission (and from which no Japanese in America would be barred) and the *kondan* backgrounders, which were not on the foreigners' agenda. The NSK also got more personal:

When a subject having a delicate bearing on Japanese-U.S. interests is under discussion, can the Cabinet Minister be expected to talk freely if American correspondents are present? . . . Japanese politicians have a unique manner of circumlocution. Can foreign correspondents adequately understand this?[13]

AT A SNAIL'S PACE

By 1972–1973 the frustrations of American reporters in Tokyo finally caught the attention of two of those binational organizations that nervously monitor the emotional temperature between the two Pacific partners. The first of these was the Shimoda III conference in June of 1972, a do-gooding confab of American and Japanese private-sector worthies traditionally held at the small seaport where Townsend Harris arrived in 1856 to open the first U.S. consulate. During the early 1970s I was the accredited Japan correspondent of the now defunct *Philadelphia Bulletin*, and I was asked by my managing editor, Dr. George Packard, a member of the American panel, to prepare a run-down of the kisha club problem for his presentation to the conferees. The American side at Shimoda III actually did raise the possibility of restricting Japanese reporters' access in Washington, but the impact of that threat was immediately defused by a flurry of promises from the Japanese panel. The Americans quickly retracted, and what followed was a dilatory sequence of half-measures over the ensuing decade—a classic example of the limited effectiveness of joint declarations by "friendship" societies and cultural-exchange groups in opening up Japan's cartels of the mind.

A similar stab at "declaration diplomacy" was made in October 1973, in Tokyo at the periodic Japan-U.S. news executives' conference sponsored by the NSK and the American committee of the Zurich-based IPI. Complaints by resident foreign journalists were led by FCCJ president Sam Jameson (*L.A. Times*) who wryly noted that, whereas Japan's import quotas were by then 97 percent liberalized to foreign goods, the liberalization rate for foreigners' access to Japan's news sessions was about two percent. It had taken seven years to open the prime minister's press conference, but no one had seven years to spend jimmying open the next source. The NSK-IPI powwow produced a joint resolution deploring the situation, and several of the Japanese executives present entered into an *informal* commitment to make *personal* efforts to present the case for greater access to officials and press clubs at major news-making institutions.[14] As an active participant in that conference, I also recall the time spent by the American correspondents in upbraiding the U.S. executives for their lack of interest in, and space for, Japan news in their own papers. As one sympathetic foreign-desk editor put it, "I want to help you—but try to keep your stories to 400–500 words!" This alleged lack of American readers' interest in Japan was one of the most powerful weapons the kisha clubs used in dismissing the complaints of Tokyo's foreign scribes.

Indeed, one month earlier the Foreign Ministry's top press official and "spokesman for Japan," Ambassador Tsutomu Wada, had already struck back with his own laundry list of problems with foreign correspondents. They couldn't speak Japanese, he told the *Sandee Mainichi* (Sunday Mainichi) magazine, they lacked the requisite personnel, and most fundamentally there was the cultural difference:

> What's the difference with Japanese reporters? Well, as all Japanese are brought up on the same cultural basis even on delicate issues, a certain degree of explanation is sufficient to obtain understanding of what's behind the matter. We may beg to leave off at a certain point, but we can't expect telepathy to work with foreign correspondents. What matters [to them] is what we say with our mouths. Their demands call for "yes" or "no" answers. . . . We can hardly expect these correspondents to understand that at times we engage in what may be called "intellectual gymnastics." On the surface, issues are often strongly opposed, but in the heart they may be entirely favored. . . . I don't think it is a matter of language barrier but of the thinking of the people. Even those foreign correspondents who have married Japanese women probably can't figure it out.[15]

Once again a Japanese critic was confusing requests for routine admission to on-the-record press events (on the simple basis of an official press card, as in Washington) with a rather precious argument about cultural incompatibility. No American sources or journalists would think of excluding Japanese correspondents from similar on-the-record opportunities because of their faulty English, shortage of staff, or non-Western psychology. Such shortcomings would simply be allowed to take their natural toll on the quality of Japanese news reporting from the United States.

Nonetheless, by the early 1970s these cumulative pressures had launched a glacier of meticulously hedged kisha club openings. As early as 1965 the press club at the Prime Minister's Office (PMO) had started admitting foreigners as "observer members" with the right to ask questions if they had prior clearance of the club captain. It was never a popular formula because of its tight restrictions even in an on-the-record setting. By 1973 regular English-language briefings for the foreign press had been instituted on a weekly basis at the Foreign Ministry and twice monthly at the Ministry of International Trade and Industry (MITI), but these remained at best a "separate-yet-equal" stopgap, catering to the linguistic laziness of the outlanders and featuring large doses of those "yes-*and*-no" dodges alluded to—and often delivered, as I recall—by Ambassador Wada. The foreign press had long since agreed that Japanese press conferences quite rightly should be held in the Japanese language exclusively and that only foreigners fluent in the tongue, or their local Japanese assistants, would presume to attend. The kisha clubs, however, were very slow to drop their claims that foreign journalists would insist on putting their questions in English or bring along interpreters, thereby crowding the space and slowing the pace of the press sessions.

By 1974, foreigners were allowed to come as *non*-members and ask questions (in Japanese, with prior permission) at the regular press sessions of the Prime Minister, Foreign Minister, MITI Minister, and Chief Cabinet Secretary, but entree to the much juicier vice-ministerial backgrounders remained off limits, as well as access to all other government agencies. There were also two events around mid-decade that served to cool relations between the foreign and Japanese press corps, thereby slowing progress on the access issue. One was the unexpected and for Prime Minister Tanaka disastrous barrage of embarrassing questions about personal finances at his late 1974 appearance before the FCCJ. The other was the opening of the Nippon Press Club's palatial premises in 1976, which siphoned off many of the visiting foreign VIPs from the relaxed and candid ambience of FCCJ press luncheons to the more ritualistic and precontrived appearances at Japan's new national press building.

The personal pique of many of Tokyo's foreign journalists was fueled less by persistent barriers at the government level than by what seemed a meanspirited monopoly of sources in every conceivable sector as they sought to cover less than world-shaking matters of interest to themselves or their home editors. One classic case was the experience of Donald Kirk of the *Chicago Tribune* in trying to interview former Japanese Imperial Army 2nd Lieut. Hiroo Onoda who had emerged from the Philippine jungles in 1974, three decades after the war. Having bought a ticket on the press car of the express "bullet" train from Tokyo to Osaka, Kirk approached the overnight hero at his seat after the photographers had finished snapping hundreds of photos only to be waved away by an angry Japanese reporter shouting "*dame desu*!" ("You mustn't do that!"). Only he, the captain in charge of the accompanying Ministry of Health and Welfare kisha club, was allowed to ask questions of Onoda. Polite entreaties being of no avail, Kirk and his Japanese interpreter managed to sneak up later for a few gleanings as the club chieftain was distracted elsewhere. "Mr. Dame Desu" soon stormed back up the aisle to demand that the intruding foreigner cease and desist. "You are not following our rules," he bellowed. As Kirk put it later in the FCCJ's journal:

> What rules? What obligation? You paid for your ticket on the train. You never heard of any rules for walking up to a guy and asking him a question. What's more, if presented with such rules, you would specifically refuse to agree to them. You recognize no "rules" other than the basic laws of the land.[16]

During the 1980s, the barring of foreign reporters from major stories became more frequent and outrageous, both in the corporate world as American correspondents found themselves unable to attend press conferences announcing dramatic

Japanese investments and takeovers in the United States, and on the political beat as a series of scandals rocked the foundations of Japan's postwar party system. At a time when trade tensions between the U.S. and Japan were going from simmer to boil, economic reporters were kept from some of the top stories of the decade:

- The press conference announcing plans by Toyota for a major automobile factory in Kentucky in 1985. The Keidanren kisha club at the Japan Federation of Economic Organizations pleaded too small a room.
- The announcements by Fujitsu of a majority stake in the American chip maker Fairchild Semiconductor and by Nippon Electric (NEC) of a joint venture with U.S. electronics giant Honeywell, as well as the press conference held in Tokyo for the U.S. Semiconductor Industries Association, all in 1986. No foreign reporters were invited, and those who got wind of these sessions were advised they could not attend.
- A similar exclusion in 1986 of European correspondents from All Nippon Airways' (ANA) announcement at the Transport Ministry kisha club of its purchase of an entire fleet of passenger jets from the Airbus consortium. Reporters from the EC countries were left to read all about it in the Japanese newspapers the following morning.
- And finally, at decade's end, as though nothing had been learned, Sony's controversial and long-awaited $3.4 billion acquisition of Columbia Pictures in October 1989, when only two foreign journalists managed to get in. In January 1990, at a good-feelings convention of the Japan-Western (U.S.) Association to which I had been invited as keynote speaker, I suggested that Sony by excluding U.S. newspeople had missed a golden opportunity to defuse American anxieties about Japan's appropriation of yet another of their cultural icons. I was trying to be helpful and had no idea that the Japanese delegation included Sony's own PR chief, who promptly retorted that no debarring had been intended and that it had all been an unfortunate "misunderstanding." *Déjà écouté.*

Frustrations in covering noneconomic issues included:

- The collapse of negotiations for coverage of Japan's Defense Agency—compared to which the Pentagon is an open house—after a Soviet reporter was unmasked in 1983 as an active spy.
- The barring of AP's picture desk man from a Simon and Garfunkel concert in Tokyo. ("It's an American group for chrissake, and here we are an American news organization which reaches virtually every corner of the earth . . . and they wouldn't let us in.")[17]
- The total exclusion of foreign reporters at the courts, National Police Agency, and Tokyo District Prosecutors' office as the lengthy Recruit scandal toppled two governments during 1987; as revelations of collusive *dango* practices in the construction industry became a major U.S. trade complaint; as ruling LDP kingmaker Shin Kanemaru went to jail on an indictment for tax evasion in 1993; and as the even greater Sagawa Kyubin scandal muddied the political waters of the early 1990s. The attitude at Japan's police and judiciary press clubs was encapsulated by the response a prosecutor gave over the phone to *L.A. Times* correspondent Andrew Horvat, who was covering the investigation by Tokyo authorities of Kazuyoshi Miura for a well-publicized murder committed in Los Angeles in 1981. Turned away at the courts, Horvat had rung up the prosecutors' office and was almost to first base in his fluent Japanese when his interlocutor suddenly broke off: "You're a *gaijin* [foreigner]? I'm not supposed to talk to you."[18]

In High Dudgeon at Last

These were the same years of financial liberalization and the "bubble" economy that witnessed the foreign lawyers' push for greater access, and in 1985–1986 the journalists—feeling that they, too, had had enough—launched a campaign of direct appeals to as many of the major Japanese kisha clubs as they felt they could spare the time and energy for. The last straw had come when they were shut out from the Narita Airport press conference given by Korea's leading opposition politician, Kim Dae Jung, on his way home to Seoul from America in February 1985. Despite the foreign correspondents' prior contacts with the U.S. office of the Japanese Christian group nominally sponsoring Kim's appearance, the Narita Airport and Commercial Broadcasters kisha clubs appropriated the event "as though it were a private party—attendance by invitation only,"[19] as the respective heads of the FPIJ and FCCJ put it in their protest letter to the NSK of April 1995 opening their campaign.

The Open Letter called for across-the-board access to all on-the-record press conferences (*kisha kaiken*) organized by the kisha clubs, citing the lack of progress over a quarter century, the impossibility of negotiating separate agreements with each of several hundred clubs, and the principle of reciprocity, reminding Japanese journalists of the far greater access they enjoyed in Western countries. That *démarche* produced a new nonbinding NSK "Guideline" of 3 September 1985, asking the clubs to cooperate with foreign reporters in whatever way possible and to allow them to participate in official on-the-record conferences. The very next day leading officers of the FPIJ and FCCJ paid a personal call on Foreign Minister Shintaro Abe, himself a former journalist, to seek his support for the faithful implementation of the new directive and to register apprehension over its appended "Notes," a retrogressive gloss recommending to the clubs the old, tightly controlled "observer member" model of the now supposedly superseded Guideline of 1978. One step forward, one step back.

Despite initial euphoria over Abe's personally expressed conviction that "this revised Guideline will lead to satisfactory results," the campaign's orchestrator, FPIJ chairman and BBC bureau chief William Horsley, was quick to vent outraged disappointment to his colleagues:

> [The] Notes read like a re-run of the old 1978 Guideline which has been the subject of all our heartaches and effort for the past 7 years. On the face of it we have been duped. We have been made to look like the dumb Yankee tourist lured into playing a card-game with the hawker outside a London tube station. . . .
>
> [We] are told it is up to us to go on pressing, and to negotiate

agreements with particular kisha clubs—a laborious and perhaps self-defeating business. . . . We must reserve the option of taking our complaint directly to the IPI ourselves. . . . Also, diplomats from some Western embassies in Tokyo have taken an active and sympathetic interest in the discrimination against the foreign press, viewing it as a problem similar to that of the freedom of foreign lawyers to conduct business in Japan. . . .

Why should Japanese journalists have opportunities for firsthand coverage which are denied to the foreign press here? I imagine that the Japanese press would be seriously inconvenienced if, for example, they were to find that their Washington correspondents had all their White House or Congressional passes withdrawn. Perhaps a special "observer membership" system might be created just for Japanese newsmen, to take effect in all capitals from Washington to Vienna![20]

By the end of 1985 not a single kisha club or government ministry had come forward to volunteer open access or even advise of more limited plans. Although cognizant of its possible futility and its contravention of FPIJ's own across-the-board ideal, Horsley (a nephew of the Earl of Devon) rallied his FCIJ/FCCJ pikemen for a broad assault on kisha club battlements in January 1986. A second FPIJ letter was drafted and hand-delivered to 31 sources and their attached clubs in Japan's bureaucracy, Diet, ruling LDP, and Keidanren, sounding out their intentions with respect to the new NSK guideline. This was followed by a round of personal visitations by foreign journalist "contact persons" to each of the major target ministries and clubs.

The Japanese responses revealed considerable ignorance and confusion about the foreigners' plight, great sensitivity about access to the informal *kondan* (which had not even been requested), and they regurgitated many of the old qualms about foreign participation. The letter for the National Police Agency club was rejected at the gate, and even the most helpfully inclined of the clubs collectively produced a parchesi board of divergent formulae, cumbersome processes, and proposed negotiations. The folly of having deadline-chasing reporters delve too deeply into this labyrinthine game soon became evident, as did the danger of mistaking (as several of the "contact persons" apparently had) a friendly reception at some clubs for a genuine breakthrough. It was during these very same months that the foreign press shut-outs at Fujitsu, NEC, and ANA occurred, necessitating yet a third letter of protest and entreaty from FPIJ Chairman Horsley in December 1986, directed this time to the business sector.

Two familiar problems where the foreign press already had some access were confirmed by these saturation contacts. With foreign correspondents barely on their radar the Japanese frequently failed to provide full and timely notification of high-priority special conferences, while foreign attendance was sporadic at the more perfunctory and marginally newsworthy regular sessions. The divergence in news focus, manpower, and logistical requirements as between a numerous and highly specialized national press corps and a small "roving" band of resident foreign generalists has been very simply solved in other free societies by giving the outsiders automatic access to all public events and leaving them (just as the locals are left) to develop deeper background contacts on their own.

Had the NSK and the clubs acceded to the FPIJ request for access to all on-the-record opportunities, the water very soon would have found its own level. That is to say, the patterns of foreign press interest and the actual flows of participating foreign journalists into a few dozen of the key kisha clubs would have become apparent in very short time, allowing those clubs to make suitable standing arrangements. In their somewhat erratic comings and goings, the foreigners would not be much different from those Japanese club members with multiple beats who only show up from time to time at any given club, although they may actually outnumber the regularly present members. But lack of a single authority and pandemic discomfort at any foreign ingress blocked implementation of the "principle" the FPIJ thought it had won assent to in 1985.

The campaign of 1985–1986 was useful as a mutually educational exercise, but concessions remained slow and piecemeal. The Foreign Ministry, impelled to set an example, had persuaded its own Kasumi Club to admit all properly accredited foreigners to its regular on-the-record conferences on a *non-*

membership basis in 1980, and toward the end of the decade some of the less critical sources like the Environment Agency followed suit. In 1989, with the rising centrality of financial news, the clubs at the Ministry of Finance, Economic Planning Agency, and Bank of Japan extended similar privileges, but only to three foreign organizations: AP-Dow Jones, Reuters, and Knight-Ridder.

By 1992–1993, as Bloomberg led the demands for admission to the Kabuto Club, pressures were building up especially from the wire services for full membership in Japan's kisha clubs. In April 1992, American embassy officials visited the NSK in support of Bloomberg. In June, the National Press Club in Washington wrote the Foreign Ministry to protest the clubs' violation of the spirit of press freedom and demand access for all foreign reporters, likening the issue to that of Japan's trade protectionism.[21] Indeed, U.S. negotiators at the bilateral Structural Impediments Initiative talks had mentioned the kisha club problem several times, and in October FCCJ president Clayton Jones (*Christian Science Monitor*), taking off the velvet gloves, suggested that, "perhaps the FCCJ can follow the tactics of the kisha clubs and threaten to boycott all news about Japan. That would provide some insight on what it's like to be shut out."[22]

All this spelled growing international embarrassment for Japan, and, true to form, the Foreign Ministry's Kasumi Club was the first to move by granting "full" membership to a select group of six: AP, Reuters, Agence France-Presse, Knight-Ridder, CNN, and a Korean television network. In order to do so it waived the first half of the Japanese press's Catch-22 requirement: that news organizations represented in the kisha clubs had to belong to the NSK, whose membership in turn was restricted to Japanese firms!

Yet another NSK Guideline was issued in June 1993 recommending that, in view of Japan's new prominence internationally, foreign correspondents who wished to join should in principle be granted full membership in the clubs—meaning of course participation in the jealously guarded informal *kondan* as well. That hopeful premise, however, was quickly eroded by the customary "Interpretation," which argued that foreigners were most likely to become "nonregular" members in practice. It suggested the establishment—once again—of an "observer membership" system, and as usual left the decision up to each of the individual kisha clubs. These, once again, were defined as being primarily social in character and in no position—so went the old refrain—to influence reportorial problems arising between the foreign press and Japanese sources.[23] Two steps forward and two steps back.

By the end of 1993, in addition to the six at the Foreign Ministry and the financial news services at the Stock Exchange, Reuters had been accepted for membership at the Economic Planning Agency's club and was being considered for admission at MITI and (along with AP-Dow Jones and Knight-Ridder) at the Finance Ministry, while AP had been accepted at the Imperial Household Agency (Kunaicho)—a "coup" that emboldened it to press for full membership at Finance, MITI, Justice, the Prime Minister's Office, and Keidanren. And, at long last, up to two foreign reporters were being accepted at most regular press conferences of the Justice Ministry, Defense Agency, and Tokyo District Prosecutor's Office.

By 1996, however, there were signs of fatigue among the foreign press as the forward line of bitterly contested foot-by-foot advances settled into the mud of exhaustion, rather like the trenches of northern France in World War I. "What's a *kondan*?" one major bureau chief asked me three years into his first Japan tour. The financial wires had been admitted to a sort of associate membership—still barring them from the *kondan* backgrounder briefings—at the five major economic sources: MITI, EPA, the Finance Ministry, the Bank of Japan, and the Stock Exchange. The Associated Press, the largest foreign news organization, however, remained a full member only at the Foreign Ministry, having settled for "observer status" at the Kunaicho and for the permission granted its staff to attend the regular press conferences (*kaiken*) on a non-member basis at the Prime Minister's Office, the Diet, the Defense Agency, and the Public Prosecutor's Office upon issuance of individual I.D. cards.

Like the smaller bureaus, the AP found the the duties of full membership—including the rotating club captaincy and a continuous physical presence—too onerous. As of 1996 the on-the-record *kaiken* of all ministries of the government except the Tokyo Metropolitan Police were in principle open to foreign correspondents *subject to* the agreement of the relevant kisha clubs. In practice this usually meant *ad hoc* permissions for each occasion from the club captains (*kanji*)—some of whom preferred to keep their doors closed—and repeated applications for attendance either by the individual foreigner or through the Japanese staff of the FCCJ. Even journalists for the financial wires, with their formal membership, have found it necessary to cultivate a friend or two among the Japanese members who could keep them alerted to important club events.

Unfortunately, the opening of some key kisha clubs to various degrees of membership for the wire services, without granting unconditional across-the-board access for all foreign newspeople to all on-the-record *kisha kaiken* of the Japanese press, left many foreign newspaper, television, and freelance reporters—including the 56 Americans posted from the U.S. as of 1995—either excluded or negotiating on a case-by-case basis. And it has taken an enormous outlay of energy on top of their regular work. It is as if Japan's 181 correspondents in the U.S. had been forced to spend decades ringing doorbells on Pennsylvania Avenue, Wall Street, and Sunset Boulevard to see only the Nikkei financial reporters and the Kyodo wire service ushered inside.[24]

There was another event in 1993 that suggests how far apart Japanese and foreign journalists remain in their basic professional values as well. In 1992 the Japanese imposed on themselves a news blackout concerning the Crown Prince's seemingly endless search for a bride—a replay of their months-long "self-restraint" on coverage of the late Emperor Hirohito's terminal illness in 1988–1989, when even to mention his possible cancer was taboo. The foreign press refused to join the ban. Agence France-Presse likened it to "a revival of wartime censorship," while Britons muttered about the bold headlines Japan's dailies were constantly flashing about the marital troubles of Prince Charles and Princess Diana.[25] In the end, the *Washington Post*, in March 1993, scooped the final choice of Japan's future

Empress, thereby forcing the Japanese to break their own silence. Bulls in the china shop, indeed.

Whereas foreign lawyers received half a loaf at the single stroke of a legislative pen and enjoyed some support from Japanese business, journalists have been subjected to the oriental torture of a thousand slices with a lukewarm Foreign Ministry as their sole Japanese ally. Nevertheless there are familiar echoes of the attorneys' struggle. The Europeans (as a high U.S. embassy official confided to me) felt they had no bargaining chips with Japan on press and cultural grievances, and thus preferred the Americans to do all the prying open, then moving snugly into the breach. The Japanese press also briefly attempted in 1990 to float the old canard of there being "similar barriers in the U.S."—conflating passing inconvenience with systematic discrimination. For example, Japanese reporters in Washington complained that they had been denied chairs and desk space at the Treasury (where they were on a first-come-first-served waiting list); that U.S. reporters at White House conferences objected to sitting next to them because they smoked too much; and that American officials often failed to provide the level of detail they wanted.[26]

Nor have Japan's news cartels been without their foreign apologists. These reporters, while not necessarily approving of the system, tend like most Japanese apologists for the clubs to take a culturally relativist position stressing—for those who can buy it—the force of social habit over deliberate discriminatory and exclusionary intent.

During the heat of battle in 1986, for example, Gebhard Hielscher (*Sueddeutsche Zeitung*) was willing to allow philosophically that, "the problem is essentially a conflict of two cultures and two opposing systems, that finds foreigners locked out—but not on purpose."[27] In 1992, Jochi University Professor Gregory Clark (formerly with *The Australian*) objected to what he saw as "yet another frontal attack on the Japanese press club system," chiding his former colleagues for failing to learn the language, to establish their own network of good news sources, and to use the enormous volume of relevant information available in published form. "It is also true," Clark admitted, "that most of the Japanese media have tribal attitudes toward news reporting, with taboos on handling certain news items and a herd mentality in reporting others. But that is a by-product of the culture, not the press club system."[28] And Reuters bureau chief Thomas Thomson, who stayed on the sidelines during David Butts's assault on the Stock Exchange club and got in ahead of Bloomberg, has been a consistent advocate of working around the clubs and taking a culturally acceptable low-key approach toward them.[29]

GO FOR BROKE?

To summarize: Japan's kisha club cartels are problematical on three counts.

1. In professional terms, a privileged group of Japanese journalists and corporate media monopolizes and regulates the flow of news, a commodity that in all other industrialized democracies would be viewed (beyond narrowly defined safeguards of national security and privacy) as an unrestricted public resource. The aptest professional analogy would be to a cabal of doctors that had managed to corner access to a nation's pharmaceutical drugs. Indeed, as with the lawyers, the odor of professional self-interest and sheer economic greed lingers on in the wake of all the explanations about "historical tradition" and "cultural difference." Even more disturbing is the blithe manner in which newspeople in a supposedly free country have arrogated to themselves the information-control functions characteristic of governments in authoritarian societies.

2. In political terms, the reporters' clubs are retrogressive, representing as they do a slightly liberalized extension of the conformist structure imposed during World War II on a more freewheeling prewar press. As an integral part of Japan's powerful administrative state, the clubs, with their mutual backscratching between reporters and sources, serve as a brake on the healthy development of Japanese democracy. What Japan's political system today requires

more than anything else is a more open and intelligent political debate, and far more transparency in the seats of power. Unfortunately, Japanese journalists and sources alike tend to view the gathering and dissemination of news as first serving the needs of public policy and national interest as defined by those in power, and only secondarily the public's right to know or the pursuit of the truth for democracy's sake. Under this dispensation journalists in Japan function less as one of the outside pressures upon policymaking than as part of the inside conveyor belt for formulating, transmitting, and carrying out policy decisions.

3. In foreign policy terms, the restrictions on non-Japanese journalists are simply unbecoming of an "information superpower" (*joho taikoku*, ever on the lips of Tokyo's media pundits) with aspirations to regional and global leadership. The adamant refusal of reciprocity, flying in the face of burgeoning international interest in Japan and relentless leaps in communications technology, can only lead to an increasingly embittered foreign press corps, whose personal frustrations are bound to affect the tone of their reporting. As the old Cold-War restraints on "getting tough" with Tokyo fade, calls for retaliatory pressures are bound to mount, especially from the U.S. press, which still has the largest economic stake in news from Asia and has been the most open and hospitable to the legions of Japanese correspondents who have hit its own shores.

What, practically speaking, might be done? What should the foreign press in Japan realistically be pushing for? The conceivable solutions are basically three: to achieve an optimum accommodation with the kisha club system on the basis of either (1) guaranteed access or (2) full membership; or, better still, (3) abolition of the system altogether.

After 35 years of begging for crumbs it is obvious that the old ad-hoc dynamic of on-and-off entreaties for incremental favors is simply too slow, to say nothing of demeaning. Foreign press leaders, from William Horsley's "big push" in 1985–1986 onward, have rightly invoked the need for uniform, across-the-board access to all the clubs based on principle rather than on interminable haggling. Unless foreign journalists enlist additional allies and raise the ante, however, they will continue to be passed from hand to hand on the merry-go-round of negotiating partners—from the NSK to the clubs to the sources, each shifting responsibility for action to the other two.

One conceivable goal would be the principle of 1985—to make all duly accredited foreign journalists eligible to attend all regular and extraordinary on-the-record press conferences of all the kisha clubs in Japan, whatever barriers the Japanese might wish to retain among themselves. That would come closest to the privileges that Japanese journalists automatically enjoy in the West, and in most of the nontotalitarian nations of the non-Western world. The repeated excuse about lack of space should not prove insoluble for an affluent "information superpower," while the foreign reporters, still excluded from the off-the-record *kondan* briefings that go with club membership, would continue to cultivate their own background channels.

Unfortunately, as the case of Bloomberg and the other financial news distributors demonstrates, the emergence of online, "real-time" communications technology makes it imperative for more and more of the media to have the immediate and unrestricted access that can be had only with an ongoing physical presence—that is to say, with the kind of full club memberships that were emerging in 1993. The need to cover a wide range of topics immediately and on the spot, rather than drawing second-hand from Japanese sources, will increasingly apply also to the major foreign dailies, television networks, and specialized media like industry magazines. With growing numbers of foreign journalists trained in the Japanese language and social ways as well as seasoned Japanese nationals on their staff, many foreign news bureaus could (if permitted) become fully functional in the more intimate *kondan* briefings as well as in the formal on-the-record *kaiken*. The full-membership approach with its access to the *kondan*, however, presents a problem much stickier than the logistical complexities of a system guaranteeing participation in all on-the-record press events. As *Washington Post* Tokyo bureau chief Thomas Reid remarked in 1993, "I'm not going to join any kisha club; I don't want to follow any rules. But the people who want to be in those clubs should have the right."[30] Or, as Tokyo-based journalist Peter Hadfield explained more fully:

> Many foreign news organizations hail these breaches of the system as a victory. I have my doubts. The kisha club system, after all, is effectively a formula for self-censorship. As far as I know, no kisha club has ever exposed a major scandal within the institution it covers, although (as kisha club members will tell you privately) scandals abound. Joining this system is the most effective way to muzzle the press.[31]

If foreign correspondents were to be granted full membership and exercise their resulting rights vigorously, the irresistible force of Western journalistic standards would soon collide with the immovable object of kisha-club news manipulation. To play the game by present Japanese rules would painfully strain the foreigners' professional ethics. Some might be tempted to become the intellectual counterpart of those American companies co-opted as junior partners to Japanese business cartels—those U.S. firms, brilliantly skewered by the Tokyo-based financial author and journalist Eamonn Fingleton, that have "succeeded" in Japan by settling for limited and noncompetitive but highly lucrative niches at the high-priced, luxury end of the market.[32] But most Western journalists would never do that, since with the news business some fundamental values—beyond mere moneymaking—are at stake. On the other hand, Japan's moving toward fewer restraints—giving the foreign bulls the run of their shop—would prove exciting, to say the least. It would force Japanese leaders (and journalists) to hear, and respond to, the questions that are most on the minds of the outside world, creating for the first time a genuinely open and nonmanipulated dialogue between Japan and its partners. It would also, for certain, destroy the kisha club system.

And that, precisely, is the only genuine solution, given the depressing track record of promised openings to date. More significantly—and well beyond the mere convenience of foreign scribes—the ultimate beneficiaries of simply dismantling the kisha clubs would be Japan's own political democracy and civil society, which desperately need the fresh air that a less self-censoring media system would pump into the ailing lungs of the nation's political discourse and public debate. These clubs, in their exclusionary and manipulative presumptions, are not a venerable "cultural" relic of the ancient Heian period, but a recent and deliberate political construct of modern Japan's totalitarian apogee—the wartime regime of Prime Minister Hideki Tojo.

Even the semi-official Foreign Press Center of Japan, which facilitates the work of briefly visiting foreign reporters and is sponsored jointly by the NSK and the Foreign Ministry, admits that "their [the kisha clubs'] problems have the same roots as those of *keiretsu*," Japan's mammoth business cartels.[33] The NSK, too, has long confessed to difficulties created by the system, strictly in Japan's own terms. After the political upheaval of mid-1993, Ichiro Ozawa, chief cabinet secretary in the new reformist cabinet of Morihiro Hosokawa, for some time insisted on calling his own press conferences, refusing to speak in club-controlled venues. And, ever since the Kobe earthquake and the Aum Shinrikyo religious cult murders that dominated the nation's news throughout 1995, the Japanese public itself has become more impatient than ever with delays, cover-ups, and other evasions of the truth, from whatever quarter.

Richard Halloran, Tokyo bureau chief consecutively for *Business Week*, the *Washington Post*, and *New York Times* in the 1960s and 1970s, once characterized the "Chrysanthemum Curtain" of the kisha clubs as "perhaps the most subtle form of censorship anywhere . . . the oldest and most easily practiced censorship—censorship at the source."[34] There is, however, no reason whatsoever why Japan at its present stage of social, economic, and political development cannot afford—and enjoy—a fully open media system. With authoritarian governments elsewhere in Asia now calling for press restrictions in the name of economic development, Confucian wisdom, innate cultural traits, or whatnot, this is no time for reporters from more liberal press traditions to encourage the Japanese to proffer Tokyo's insidiously sophisticated system for news control as a model for their Asian neighbors. Foreign journalists do so inadvertently, however, whenever they acquiesce in Japanese restrictions, be it through inertia or misplaced cultural sensitivity. And that leads to the final bullet that Western journalists find so hard to bite—the very idea of retaliatory sanctions.

The pursuit by the foreign press community in Japan of any of the three foregoing solutions will be strenuously resisted by the kisha clubs and their government and corporate supporters. Persistent appeals from foreign embassies and from news organizations like the International Press Institute, the American Society of Newspaper Editors, and national and overseas press clubs throughout the free world may serve as a starter. But they will almost certainly require further leveraging with some judiciously targeted, highly symbolic retaliatory pressures along lines already suggested—such as withdrawing or severely restricting the press passes of Japanese correspondents to key governmental institutions in Washington and other capital cities around the globe.

A monitory package of "Japanese-style" restrictions applied to Japanese journalists overseas may be an unavoidable step for a society like Japan's where, absent a strong sense of abstract principles, issues often have to be personalized to be properly understood—that is to say, directly experienced and related to one's own daily life. To that end, such measures would have to go beyond mere threats, so easily circumvented, and actually be imposed for a meaningful period of time until the counter-pain started to sink in—I should think, for at least one year. Tenderminded Americans are certain to demur that none of this is very nice, nor very American. Even five years, however, would be but a fraction of the decades during which U.S. newspeople have had to endure—and continue to endure—far more pervasive barriers in Japan.

The time, in other words, has now come to disabuse Japan's newspeople of their conceit, so well phrased by a Japanese reporter in 1986, that, "You have your system and we have ours. That's life. Who is to say what is fair and what isn't? Just because your system is convenient for foreigners doesn't mean that ours has to be too."[35] Unfortunately, while probably nothing short of a coordinated boycott of Japanese correspondents in major world capitals is likely to move Tokyo's press toward genuine reciprocity, such measures—which seem particularly petty in a profession devoted to information and ideas—remain repugnant to the West's own liberal values. So the Japanese media continue to benefit from Western openness and universalism while drawing the pleas of cultural particularism and autonomy—in effect, a cultural right to double standards—over their own tightfistedness.

We shall find that same powerful conceit is deeply embedded in Japan's other great intellectual institution—the groves of academe.

3

ACADEMIC APARTHEID
The Peripheral Professoriate

In much the same spirit as Bloomberg at the Tokyo stock exchange, a group of seven present and former foreign teachers at Japan's national universities—having decided that they, too, should stand up—spent a busy day on 4 April 1995, publicizing an ongoing wave of dismissals of senior foreign staff at Japan's state-run institutions of higher learning. Responding to an invitation to present their complaints to the American Embassy, they led off with a press conference luncheon at the FCCJ, spent exactly one hour relating their individual cases to a visibly shaken Ambassador Walter Mondale, then watched themselves as the subject of a six-minute special on NHK's seven o'clock prime time news hour that evening. That same week the newly launched opinion monthly *Ronza* carried in its May 1995 issue an article in Japanese that I had submitted on "Apartheid at Japan's National Universities" ("Nihon no Kokuritsu Daigaku ni aru Aparutoheito").

Anxiety and consternation had been spreading throughout the foreign professoriate at national universities since December of 1992. In that month the Ministry of Education (Monbusho) issued a directive threatening budgetary sanctions against universities that insisted on retaining *gaikokujin kyoshi* (foreign instructors) who had reached the two highest pay grades. From

1893 to 1983 the *kyoshi* system was the only category under which non-Japanese could be hired at national universities. As of 1995 there were 386 *kyoshi* serving on one-year renewable contracts as language teachers or in disciplinary fields like politics or economics. Out of sixty responses to a questionnaire sent by a sympathetic Japanese law firm in mid-1994 to 145 *kyoshi* teaching English language and British and American literature, 70 percent of those over age 45 reported that they had received termination notices.[1] By the end of 1995 over 40 of these senior-level *kyoshi* had already been, or soon were to be, dismissed from positions many of them had held for as long as ten to fifteen years.

The *Asahi Shinbun* of 22 June 1993 reported that most universities had taken the directive to mean that they should get rid of *kyoshi* over the age of 50 who were in the two upper salary brackets. The Monbusho has effectively ruled out hiring any new *kyoshi* over the age of 35, and even those in their early forties with nearly a decade's service are now being dismissed. Some of the *kyoshi*, under threat of immediate dismissal, have signed agreements to move on after one or two years. It is as though the U.S. Department of Education had ordered the leading U.S. universities to ease out all non-Americans in their forties and fifties. And Japan has the second largest system of higher education (after the U.S.) in the industrialized democracies.

One explanation offered by the Monbusho to a high American Embassy official was that young Yanks would be more representative of contemporary American culture. One wonders what the Japanese would say if major American universities sent packing their senior tenured Japanese scholars because they failed to reflect the *wakamono bunka*, or "youth culture," of Tokyo's trendy Harajuku district.

The experiences of *kyoshi* responding to the survey were depressingly consistent. Virtually all had been given verbal assurances by their Japanese administrators and colleagues when they joined that they could stay on indefinitely as long as their performance was satisfactory, and that the one-year renewable contract was a mere administrative formality. Some had bought homes on the strength of those promises. Others were being thrown out a year or two short of the 17 years' service required for their pensions, with no return of their mandatory monthly payments into the fund. Faced with a late-career choice of working a double load of part-time jobs to stay in Japan or boarding a jet home to an all but nonexistent market for their talents, all found themselves abandoned in the end by their Japanese colleagues who passed the buck to the university administrators, who in turn claimed to be helpless before the Monbusho. Two comments from the survey catch the universal sense of disbelief and outrage:

(1) *Gaikokujin kyoshi*, regardless of length of service, are marginal adjuncts of the school and are subject to the whims of other English staff and administration in a way that Japanese citizens are not. This is spelled out in the contract, but in the light of treatment of Japanese nationals at foreign universities, it is definitely unfair.

(2) I have taught at Asian universities for almost 30 years but never before have I been treated so badly as by the Japanese Ministry of Education. It has broken trust. It has breached a "gentleman's agreement." But then *gaijin* are not even men, let alone gentlemen: they are "things." The Monbusho has disgraced Japan.[2]

The *kyoshi* who appeared before the NHK and FCCJ cameras on April 4 were a very brave minority. Most of the foreigners getting the academic axe had talked themselves into silence and inaction (with an occasional assist from their Japanese spouses or relatives) for fear of jeopardizing their search for new jobs. Gagging their own gullets on the way to the guillotine, they failed to raise the sort of public protest that would have been second nature to them in the West, or even if they had been working in a non-communist Chinese or Korean culture. With that, they had become more Japanese than the Japanese, afraid in any way to seem obstreperous or to offend—and, in the end, their own worst enemy.

As someone with ties to scholars, diplomats, lawyers, and journalists, I found myself cast, in the words of NHK, as a sort of senior advisor or "encourager" of the small activist group. I had served as a *kyoshi* at Tsukuba National University from

1984 to 1987 and had recently won compensation against my own dismissal by a private university. My concern over the marginalizing of foreign scholars in Japan, however, went back to my duties as the associate executive director and Japan representative of the U.S. government's Japan-U.S. Friendship Commission. During 1977–1984, when I held this post promoting bilateral cultural exchanges, official Japan was loudly announcing the imminent "internationalization" of its professoriate. The contrast between that and what I witnessed later when I actually taught at three Japanese campuses from 1984 to 1993 was simply too great to ignore. Especially striking to me were the parallels with commercial market-opening issues—the same glacial pace of progress, the absence of political will, and (one was driven to conclude) a lack of any real intention to change.

The efforts of the *kyoshi* group to advance the issue on diplomatic, parliamentary, and legal fronts during 1995 and 1996 illustrate the difficulty of changing the bureaucratically sanctioned intellectual order in Japan.[3]

"This stuff makes me cry for Japan," Ambassador Mondale sighed to his American, British, and German *kyoshi* visitors on April 4, as he wondered aloud how Japan could ever fulfill its global responsibilities if it maintained such a narrow posture toward foreign scholars and students. The embassy put out a supportive press release that evening and wrote the Monbusho seeking explanations, including the prospects for compensating those Americans released without pension. In replying the ministry was silent on pensions, admitted to having encouraged national universities to hire younger foreigners in the interest of economy, but denied—with brazen disingenuousness—that its "guidance" (*shido*) had implied any dismissals of older staff, throwing the sole responsibility for that on the universities.[4] Like the journalists, the *kyoshi* were being tossed around a triangle of unaccountability—from colleagues to university officials to the Monbusho and back.

Although by mid-1995 Mondale had spoken out publicly six times on the scholars' issue, his embassy cultural staff (the U.S. Information Service, Japan) chose to accept the Monbusho position at face value, apparently in order to win the ministry's small concession on American student access described in the following chapter. At its January 1995 session in Tokyo the intergovernmental U.S.-Japan Conference on Cultural and Educational Interchange (CULCON) had refused to take up this issue because they were looking for exchange barriers with "more resonance and specificity" that did not entail any "regulatory or policy changes" on the part of the Japanese[5]—something that would have brought a hearty guffaw from any seasoned U.S. trade negotiator. As divulged to me a year later, the Japanese side at the January 1995 session had actually threatened to close down CULCON altogether if the Americans insisted on placing the professors' issue on the agenda.

In April 1995, the Friendship Commission at its board meeting in Washington also turned down the recommendation of its Vice Chairman, Glen S. Fukushima, for a statement in support of Mondale—the comfortably tenured American professors of Japanese Studies on the board insisting that the ambassador was already doing enough. The Commission, having wound down its former two-way mission toward both countries to concentrate on educating Americans about Japan, was now "blind to this issue," and "blind to institutional matters in Japan."[6]

Nonetheless, by July 1995, LDP Dietman Hideo Usui (who was to become head of the Defense Agency in 1996) had called two high Monbusho officials to his office to demand explanations. That autumn, the Japanese lawyer who had served me so well, Shigeru Sheena, succeeded in securing a one-year reprieve from dismissal for an outspoken American *kyoshi*, Sharon Vaipae—a 54-year-old single mother with two children in Japanese primary school, who had written to six members of the U.S. Congress. From December, Sheena's office began serving on a *pro bono publico* basis as the secretariat of our protest group on behalf of dismissed or threatened foreign academics, now informally organized as Teachers Against Discriminatory Dismissals (TADD).

On 29 February 1996, ten members of TADD called on the new Parliamentary Vice Minister for Education Kiyoko Kusakabe, a member of the Upper House from the Social

Democratic Party of Japan (SDPJ, formerly Japan Socialist Party), and presented a petition requesting: (1) pensions for *kyoshi* already dismissed after many years' service; (2) the continuation of those presently scheduled for dismissal; and (3) nondiscriminatory personnel policies for foreign staff in the future. Vice Minister Kusakabe, who had studied at the London School of Economics when it was headed by a German national (Ralf Dahrendorf) heard the group out sympathetically for an hour and a half in the presence of a fellow M.P., Atsushi Nishikoori (Lower House, Sakigake Party), who promised to take the petition to the relevant Diet committees.

On 25 March 1996, Ambassador Mondale called on then Minister of Education Mikio Okuda to express directly his concern about the career insecurity of foreign teachers at national universities, and the overwhelming imbalance in the number of Japanese scholars working in the U.S. as opposed to American academics in Japan. On 7 and 21 May, Minister Okuda and the head of the Ministry's Higher Education Bureau submitted to a full hour's questioning on this issue in the Education Committee of the Upper House by Kazuto Kamiyama of the SDPJ. Referring to Mondale's concern, and to Japan's loss of international trust thanks to charges of academic "apartheid" in *Ronza* magazine, Kamiyama asked why the Ministry had to maintain a discriminatory system at the very time it was "trumpeting the call for '*kokusaika, kokusaika*,' and the internationalization of education."[7]

On 12 June, the TADD group was invited back to receive a negative reply from the visibly embarrassed but bureaucratically powerless Parliamentary Vice Minister Kusakabe. At this second meeting, the Monbusho refused outright to consider any pensions for the senior *kyoshi* previously fired; declined to rescind, or admit responsibility for, any impending dismissals in response to its 1992 guidance, arguing as always that it was entirely up to each university; and made no commitments toward a less discriminatory system. Ignoring both the pleas of the American ambassador and the sharp questioning in the Diet, the Ministry stood pat on the two minimal, cosmetic steps it had taken in a directive dated 6 November 1995—well before the events just described. In this directive, the universities were instructed to engage younger persons wherever possible as new foreign hires, and to make unmistakably clear to incoming foreign teachers the limited term of their appointment. As for the existing foreign staff, universities were urged to take into account not only age but also performance in deciding what to do with them.

The now obligatory warning to new hires that they cannot expect to stay on for very long is an extraordinarily clumsy way of encouraging the best people to come teach in Japan. Indeed, when a *kyoshi* recruiting team from Chiba National University brandished the new admonition at the University of Leipzig (their sister school), not a candidate was to be found. Young scholars apparently decided it would be safer to secure or hang on to posts in the shaky academic market of former East Germany.

For the moment, the Monbusho had delivered an effective "No" not only to foreign teachers but to the entire U.S. executive branch as represented by Ambassador Mondale. Fortunately, overseas knowledge of this issue was also seeping into the legislative track. In February 1996, a U.K. member of the TADD group of fired or threatened teachers received a strong public letter of support from the British Ambassador, David Wright, who mentioned that Member of Parliament Alastair Goodlad, then Minister of State for Foreign and Commonwealth Affairs, had raised the matter with the Japanese Vice Minister for Foreign Affairs during a visit to Tokyo in May 1995.[8] And, as of the autumn of 1996, Senators William Roth (R-Delaware) and Jeff Bingaman (D-New Mexico) had drafted and were waiting for an opportunity to present a nonbinding Senate resolution. The resolution's purpose is:

> To state the sense of the Senate concerning the Government of Japan recognizing American college and university branch campuses in Japan as American institutions of higher learning [see Chapter 4, below]; and concerning the Government of Japan's discriminatory treatment toward and termination of long-term serving foreign educators at Japan's national universities.[9]

In his own research, attorney Sheena had cut through the statutory thicket to discover the extraordinary legal Catch-22 in which the *kyoshi* were caught. Because the courts treat all teachers at national universities as officials of the Japanese state (*kokka komuin*), foreign *kyoshi* are not entitled to the protections of the Labor Standards Act (Rodo Kijun Ho) governing the private sector. Under the Labor Standards Act there are judicial precedents for arguing that repeated renewals of one-year contracts beyond a certain point create a right to continuing employment. Thus the foreign *kyoshi* have absolutely no chance of winning a suit in court since the State is free to terminate them at the end of any annual contract. Of course the foreigners are not really civil servants with all the privileges and life-tenured security of the Japanese professoriate. As an official of the National Personnel Authority (Jinji-In) put the distinction to Ellen Oki, one of the German *kyoshi*, who had lost her post at Chiba: "You are nothing but a 'part-time full-timer'" (*hijokin no jokin*)—a nonsensical contradiction in terms.

But, then, as Sheena once put it to me, we are dealing here with an unreconstructed relic of prewar Japan's old Bismarckian bureaucratic heritage that managed to slip through the postwar reforms—the absolute command of the State over its officialdom. Digging down to the deepest stratum in the October 1996 issue of *Ronza*, he concludes that the resistance to tenuring Western scholars rests on a fear of the much larger pool of resident Koreans laying claim to a wide range of public-service positions—and that, beneath it all, lies the ultimate inability or unwillingness of the Japanese to conceive of a culturally and ethnically plural nation.[10]

BIRDS OF PASSAGE

The current dismissals of senior foreign *kyoshi* are only the tip of an iceberg of academic insularity the layered depths of which we must now plumb. They rest on a century of ideological justification of the segregated *gaikokujin kyoshi* system—an academic version of the old Deshima Island in Nagasaki harbor, where the Dutch during the Tokugawa seclusion were allowed to maintain the sole Western trading post. Japan continues to deny permanent tenure to all but a handful of foreign professors at the national universities even though a new *gaikokujin kyoin* ("foreign staff") system was introduced in 1982 to permit such integration. Attitudes at the private universities are similar, partly because the Monbusho also funds and regulates them in various ways.

But let us pause for a moment to ask: Why are these esoteric goings-on behind ivied walls of any practical consequence to Japan's relations with the outside world?

For one thing, Japan's defensive attitude toward foreign participation in its internal intellectual activity is nowhere more clearly on display than in the continuing reluctance to accept non-Japanese scholars (including Japan-born Koreans and Chinese) into university teaching and research positions in a professionally standard manner—that is to say with identical duties and rights, including the fundamental right, beyond some point in service, to continuing employment or "tenure." Well over a century after the founding of Japan's first university (Tokyo) in 1877 the foreign academic in Japan remains a bird of passage—a brief "exchange" visitor, in effect, or, even if resident for decades, often caught in a revolving door of short-term contractual appointments.

Japan's academic cartel of the mind has a pedigree much older than those for lawyers or journalists, stretching back more than a hundred years to 1893. It is the cartel with the most clearcut intellectual and ideological implications, and the category (along with students) that shows the greatest nonreciprocity with the U.S. in terms of relative numbers of citizens allowed to participate in each other's respective system. It is the cartel that has been subjected to the liveliest parliamentary debate in Japan with the enactment of a major new piece of legislation, as well as the one with the most promises given and broken as that legislation was eviscerated in practice—making it the cartel for which the slogan of *kokusaika* ("internationalization") has been most flagrantly abused.

It is, furthermore, the cartel against which the foreign parties have been weakest—pathetically so—inasmuch they work *within* Japanese organizations, and are beholden to them (unlike the *gaiben* attorneys or foreign reporters) for their very livelihood and careers. Foreign teachers in Japan have also lacked their own powerful organizations like the FCCJ/FPIJ or overseas supporters on the order of the ABA or IPI, and have received little attention from their own embassy cultural staffs. Many of these foreign scholars have committed themselves to Japan for life and have settled down with their Japanese spouses and Japan-acculturated children in provincial towns or ordinary urban neighborhoods—far from Tokyo's glittering ghettos for employees of foreign embassies, corporations, news bureaus, or legal firms. As such, they have been the most directly exposed to the actual sentiments of the Japanese toward foreign co-workers, and the patent job discrimination they endure adds an inescapable human aspect to the story of this cartel.

Most significantly, the absence of integrated foreign faculty impedes a genuine two-way intellectual flow between Japan and the rest of the world because the traffic at universities is precisely in ideas. The contacts are continuous and personal with an unmediated impact on young Japanese minds, and the cachet of full professional equality—were it ever to be granted—would assure foreign scholars not only a dialogue among equals with their Japanese colleagues but also, through entree to Japan's media, a certain degree of participation in the broader debates of the nation.

For the United States, this imbalance in academic employment opportunities has had a subtle if largely unno- ticed impact on political, trade, and historical issues (e.g., on interpretations of the Pacific War), by giving Japan a stronger rhetorical footing in America than the U.S. enjoys in Japan. Japanese scholars at U.S. universities do not necessarily take Tokyo's position on bilateral issues under contention, but the respect attaching to their professional status gives them access to American scholars and opinion makers, providing Japan with an "embedded" intellectual presence in the U.S. for which there is absolutely no American equivalent in Japan. American scholars in Japan who could provide a stronger intellectual presence—having been around long enough to handle the Japanese language well and acquire other accessory skills—are barred from respectable academic niches and nor- mally return to the U.S. after the first whack of the revolving door if they are set on serious academic careers. That leaves the briefly visiting American academic superstar—who normally knows little of Japan, gets whirled around on a magic carpet of sedulous attention, and recrosses the Pacific having left hardly a dent behind.

For Japan, its rejection of human variety and vitality based not on professional qualifications but on a simplistic national/ethnic criterion, deprives Japanese universities not only of the intellectual talent that Western schools seek internationally, but also of the good will and social interchange with intellectual elites abroad that Japan badly needs in meeting its burgeoning international responsibilities. Japanese in favor of genuinely integrating foreign professors have argued that they would stimulate and challenge the Japanese staff. Others, making the same point backhandedly, have confessed that the real resistance derives from the fear many Japanese scholars still have of foreign competition. They worry (rightly or wrongly) that the outlanders might publish more frequently, cancel fewer classroom lectures, or even stir up too much intellectual controversy. Still others trot out the old bromide that non-Japanese scholars (like non-Japanese reporters) would never fit in socially.

Finally, the university is the most critical player in the broader cultural ties with other countries—as the originator, repository, and transmitter of a people's intellectual heritage; as the institution that forms the leadership of any modern state and is in turn reshaped by it; as a seminal influence on the school system and mass media; and as a seat of learning and a social community. Courses about other nations and cultures and the short-term presence of foreign students, exchange professors, and visiting researchers all add to the cosmopolitan flavor of a campus. Most essential, however, are the permanently tenured foreign staff who through their teaching, writing, and full participation as colleagues make a continuing, long-term contribution.

In the "late-modernizing" Meiji state, unlike many of the former colonial "developing" countries of the postwar period, Japan's political leadership was in place well ahead of the educational institutions it proceeded to fashion out of whole cloth—with starkly utilitarian goals of national military and economic strength in mind. Anyone who thinks that what happens in Japanese academe is an abstruse matter unrelated to current trade issues today should bear in mind the strong links between universities and political purpose throughout Japan's modern century.

THREE ACADEMIC CLOSED SHOPS

Japan's university system is the second largest in the advanced industrial world after the U.S., boasting 2.5 million undergraduate and graduate students at 565 universities (excluding two-year junior colleges) in 1995. Their external aspect, both physical and organizational, would be familiar to any American visitor, although several important differences would emerge after a brief stay.

At its most visible level, the university in Japan is nonresidential. Be it a grimy, crowded, urban plot inherited from the prewar period or one of the palatially designed and landscaped new suburban settings, the Japanese campus sucks in its thousands of students and scholars by day like a bellows, then collapses into eerie desolation at night. Instead of the manifold undergraduate departments of a typical American faculty of arts and sciences, Japanese universities contain a small number of powerful faculties of letters, law, medicine, political economy, and natural sciences. In this they resemble continental European universities, although these faculties' truculent autonomy vis-à-vis each other and the university administration itself would have startled even a German academic of Bismarck's time. If a Westerner stayed a bit longer on a Japanese campus he or she would sense that the average Japanese student's scholarly, athletic, and social endeavors were all focused less on what Americans would call personal development and expression than on networking toward a post-graduation job with the most prestigious employer possible. The presence of so many professors working at their own alma mater would also be striking. But the oddest thing of all would be the scarcity of foreign students and—apart from the floating crowd of young part-time foreign drill-masters at the language lab—the minuscule number of foreign professorial staff.

As of 1995 there were only 3,858 foreigners among the 137,464 full-time staffers at all Japanese universities, a scant 2.8 percent. Of these foreigners, 2,304 were to be found in the private sector, 1,312 at national universities, and 242 at prefectural and municipal universities. In a breakdown by nationality at national universities in 1994 there were 97 Americans among the 371 foreign *kyoshi*, and 72 out of 389 in the new category of foreign *kyoin*, for a total U.S. share of 22.2 percent. For more nuanced proportions as to status, there were at the rank of professor and associate professor 321 foreigners among a total of 34,231 at national universities in 1995, and 1,245 among a total of 44,264 at the private schools—about .94 and 2.8 percent, respectively.[11]

There are three rooms, so to speak, in Japan's closed shop for foreign scholars: the old *gaikokujin kyoshi* ("foreign instructor") and the new *gaikokujin kyoin* ("foreign staff") systems at the national schools; and the less uniform and restrictive practices in the private sector.

GAIKOKUJIN KYOSHI

Japan's national universities (*kokuritsu daigaku*) provide the litmus test for any evaluation of its recent claims to have "internationalized" its halls of ivy. They are vastly more prestigious than the private universities (*shiritsu daigaku*) and continue to monopolize access to the higher bureaucracy and much of Japan's blue-ribbon corporate world. Their restrictions on foreign professors are system-wide and deliberate, having been made explicit in statutory regulations and official justifications; and their governmental tie makes them more indicative than the private universities of the attitudes and intentions of Japan's leadership.

Under the century-old *kyoshi* system foreign teachers enjoy an approximately 15 percent higher salary, but are denied professorial titles, participation in departmental and faculty meetings, the supervision of dissertations (the crowning task of the scholar-as-teacher), permanent job security, and other rights and duties pertaining uniformly to the Japanese staff. Ranging in effect from professors to lecturers but all lumped together as *kyoshi*, they serve on one-year renewable contracts in a generously remunerated but separate, inferior, and short-term academic echelon. Even today the 386 *kyoshi* are best seen as the equivalent of foreign technical advisors in Third World developing countries—as transitory, disposable transmitters of foreign knowledge or techniques—rather than as fellow laborers in the ongoing quest for human knowledge. They have never been the genuine scholarly reciprocal of those numerous Japanese academics employed by universities in other advanced industrial countries.

Nothing sets these teachers apart more clearly than their official designation. The jab comes not with the first term, *gaikokujin*, meaning "foreigner," but with the second. *Kyoshi* is a rather low-level, generic term for "teacher" or "instructor," bereft of academic or scholarly flavor, burdened with the pejorative nuances of "pedagogue" or "schoolmaster," and applied most typically to primary school teachers, flower-arranging or judo masters, and language instructors. The latter is what many of Japan's foreign faculty actually become, whatever their disciplinary background or achievement. Denied admission to faculty councils and other academic meetings, these "pedagogues" have been barred from positions of administrative leadership and have no voice at all in matters of personnel or curriculum—a major motive behind the original ordinance of 1893. Their salary advantage today is a bare fraction of the whopping differentials that induced foreigners to come when Japan's standard of living lagged well behind that of the West.

The most essential point of discrimination is that of temporary as opposed to permanent status. Despite the fact that the *kyoshi* pay full Japanese national and local taxes and contribute to their own retirement fund, they cannot collect their pension—or recover their contributions to it—unless they manage to last out a full seventeen years. The anomaly of their employment status has been magnified by the fact that regular Japanese academic "staffers" (*kyoin*) at both national and private universities become "tenured" in the American sense of the term—that is to say, permanently employed—from the moment they receive a full-time appointment.

Japanese universities do not have a sorting system based on

a period of apprenticeship followed by peer review leading to tenure. Permanent appointments are made, generally around the age of 30, based on scholarly record and promise and, almost always at the better universities, on some previous connection with the hiring institution or its incumbent staff. These non-term-limited appointments are customary rather than contractual, being based on a simple order of appointment, but once ensconced the Japanese scholar cannot be fired short of criminal conduct or serious ethical lapses involving the honor of the school.

The cumulative result of all these differences has been the almost total bifurcation of native and foreign academic communities in Japan. On the one hand a snugly ingrown Japanese faculty, riddled with personalism and factionalism in the absence of peer pressures to perform, jealously guards its lifetime-security cocoon against outside intrusions. On the other, there is a ghettoized expatriate professoriate speaking only to one another, remote from the pressing issues of Japanese education, viewed by their students as a bit of fashionable exotica and by the Japanese staff as a token of *kokusaika*. Some of them pursue serious research despite their isolation while others simply draw their salaries in order to support a career centered on off-campus literary or artistic activities.

GAIKOKUJIN KYOIN

The current ageist assault on seasoned *gaikokujin kyoshi* comes on top of a failure to genuinely integrate foreign scholars with regular Japanese staff under the new *gaikokujin kyoin* (foreign "staffer") system mandated by the Diet in 1982 as a means of "internationalizing" the national universities. The new "Kyoin Law"[12] of 1982 authorized the appointment of foreign scholars at Japanese national and "public" (i.e., prefectural and municipal) universities on terms identical to those for the full-time Japanese teaching staff (known as *kyoin*), but with one enormous exception that quickly undermined the original purpose and spirit of the law. Although intended by its original sponsors to provide permanent employment similar to that of Japanese professors, and widely advertised as offering academic "tenure" to foreigners, the law as finally passed left the question of tenure to the discretion of each university.

Thirteen years later, as of 1995, only 66 (or 14.3 percent) of the 461 foreign *kyoin* had been given open-ended, non-term-limited posts similar to those held by their Japanese colleagues. Of Japan's 98 national universities and their 19 joint-use research facilities, only one, Tokyo University, has adopted permanent tenure in principle for its foreign *kyoin*. The others introduced regulations forbidding or strongly discouraging such hires, opting instead for short-term contract periods, averaging about three years. This is as if each of the fifty U.S. states had agreed to give job security to approximately one non-American scholar. Or to two, considering the twice-larger U.S. population.

The 1982 law led to cheery announcements by certain schools that they were now ready to "tenure foreign scholars with exactly the same salary, titles, duties and rights as we Japanese—and a three-year contract into the bargain!" A contract with a fixed term, however, is not "tenure," and a post without job security can hardly be considered the equal of one that provides it. The 85 percent of the new-system foreign *kyoin* who are on contracts now enjoy academic titles and the privilege of attending interminable faculty meetings, but they have very little clout in academic management since they are entirely dependent on the good will of Japanese colleagues for their contract renewals. They remain as vulnerable to sudden and arbitrary dismissal as the old-system *kyoshi*. Legally speaking, their average three-year contract *periods* (for which they have been *academically* approved) represent a chain of one-year contracts, and cases have come to my attention of newly arrived younger *kyoin* who have been given terminal three-year contract periods—in for one nonrenewable stint, then out.

The total figure of 66 tenured foreign *kyoin* at national universities as of 1995 is somewhat misleading in that it includes a number of resident Koreans (or even former Japanese nationals) who were born and educated through university level in Japan. It also bears mentioning that a considerable proportion of the *kyoin* serve at the less prestigious provincial campuses, teaching language-related courses, and are virtually indistinguishable from the old-system *kyoshi*.

PRIVATE UNIVERSITIES

Since the Ministry of Education not only subsidizes some 30 percent of the budget of Japan's private universities but also authorizes changes in the complement of students and staff for any given department as well as all additions of new departments or physical plant, it is not surprising that the restrictive policies toward foreign instructors at national universities have begun to spill over into the private sector. By 1995, for example, even a well-known Christian academy in the southern island of Kyushu reportedly had begun firing its long-standing missionary teachers and was setting its new hiring age limit at 30.

Indeed, in November 1995, the University Deliberative Council (Daigaku Shingikai), an advisory panel to the education minister, proposed that private universities be encouraged to place their foreign professors on term-limited contracts as was being done at the national schools. That drew no audible objection, but in October 1996, the council provoked anguished protest from scholars nationwide when it recommended the introduction of fixed-term hires for the Japanese staff as well, as a means of limbering up the ossified tenure-upon-entry system at both national and private universities. Since the decision was to be left to each institution, there was still some question as to the seriousness or feasibility of the proposed "optional contract system" for Japanese.[13]

Given the intense factionalism and personal grudges that have festered in the hothouse of mutually assured job security, one might reasonably suppose that any enforcement of peer-decreed term limits for incumbent Japanese professors would quickly lead to mutual logrolling—if not to mutual cashiering, leaving no one to teach the students. In the title of its editorial for 24 October 1996, *Nature* magazine characterized the hubbub among Japanese academics over the possible loss of permanent positions while denying such posts to foreigners as "Tenured Hypocrisy." Many observers took it as a license to expel leftists. Some assumed it would only apply to incoming staff, if it were implemented at all. With the council's real purpose as yet unclear, we can only speculate as to whether the ousters of foreign staff may be serving as a trial run. In any case, a universal system of term appointments would ultimately be controlled not by scholarly peers but by the Monbusho and its compliant campus administrators—an enormously regressive political and ideological step, were that to come.

Japan's private universities differ from the national schools less in their attitude toward foreign scholars than in the absence of any system-wide rules for employing them. Nearly all of their full-time non-Japanese staff—although enjoying the traditional academic titles and sometimes participating in faculty meetings—are there on renewable annual contracts, often strung out indefinitely but never proof against a sudden capsizing. Highly qualified scholars have been abruptly dropped after lengthy years of service, or shunted about from one private campus to another at the end of each contractual period.

There is one critical contrast with the national universities, and that is that employees at private institutions are not considered officials of the Japanese state. Hence, they can sue for redress under the Labor Standards Act, and during 1996, several long-term foreign teachers who had been summarily dismissed from private universities took their cases to court or were considering doing so. Two American professors were suing at the Nagoya and Asahikawa district courts, assisted by aggressive lawyers and with broad collegial support. Rebecca Pickett, a Ph.D. in her mid-60s supporting a husband over 70, had been promised her post until age 68 at the newly-founded Shizuoka Institute of Science and Technology. Gwendolyn Gallagher had been fired after twelve years of full-time teaching at Asahikawa University, where her Japanese husband also works as a professor, on the simple grounds (as conveyed to the judge) that the department wanted to "refresh" its staff with foreign teachers who had not been in Japan "too long" to teach about their home country effectively.

The only two schools with a significant proportion of their foreign staff in lifetime posts are the Jesuit-operated Jochi (Sophia) University with its naturally "tenured" foreign scholar-priests, and the Protestant-affiliated International Christian University with its dual-language curriculum and parallel Japanese and foreign staffs. Both are in Tokyo, and both are the exceptions that prove the rule. Far more typical are Japan's two premier private universities. Waseda, with over 40,000 students and 900 Japanese staff in 1994, had 16 foreign teachers tenured in the language-teaching sections of several of its faculties, while Keio (over 25,000 students and 1,000 staff) had 13 tenured foreigners in a similar capacity. With one or two exceptions, neither university as yet has any tenured foreign professors teaching the prestigious upper-division *senmon* (disciplinary speciality) courses or giving the capstone Junior-Senior seminars.[14]

There are indeed more foreign teachers at private than at national universities, but a large majority of them are part-time hires. Like most of the full-time regulars, they are specialists in language and/or literature, teaching and working entirely in their own native tongue, with only tangential social and intellectual contact with their Japanese colleagues. This ghetto phenomenon runs through the private system like an archipelago, and may well be a psychologically comfortable arrangement for some people on both sides. But it is a pity that so few attempts have been made to integrate the rarer foreign academic capable of teaching a substantive disciplinary (i.e., non-language) subject, and with a command of Japanese sufficient for lecturing and for full participation in the administrative business of the university.

It is as if American universities had never hired a Chinese prodigy to teach physics or a Spaniard like Santayana to teach philosophy, and engaged Germans only to give conversational drill or (if they had fancy degrees from Tuebingen or Heidelberg) to lecture on Goethe and Schiller to advanced concentrators in Germanistik—and then set up special common rooms, never trodden by the Yankee staff, where they could mingle with Portuguese, Koreans, and Arabs, also there only to teach their own native tongue.

In all of the advanced industrial nations of Western Europe, North America, and the British Commonwealth, university appointments have generally been open to all qualified comers for the past quarter century. American and Commonwealth universities have long recruited on a world-wide basis. France has often been cited by the Japanese as another administrative state where university staff, as civil servants, are required to possess French nationality. But even in France, with the reforms following the great campus upheavals of the late 1960s, foreign scholars are now eligible for all but the top administrative posts. Similarly in former West Germany—where professors were public officials of the individual states (Laender)—all restrictions had been lifted by the 1970s on the employment and advancement of foreign scholars into any teaching or administrative post.[15]

Full comparative statistics for Japanese and other foreign nationals in long-term service at European and American institutions of higher learning are unavailable because Western universities, unlike those in Japan, do not officially distinguish between native and foreign faculty members, much less keep statistical breakdowns for tenured versus contractual foreign staff. The listing maintained by the Institute of International Education, for example, does not distinguish between foreigners on the teaching faculty as opposed to researchers, and its figure of 58,075 foreign scholars (including 5,155 Japanese) at American universities for the academic year 1994–1995 covers only those on temporary "J" or "H" visas—that is to say, short-term "visiting" or "exchange" professors and others on fixed-term visas, omitting all those who hold "green cards" for the permanent residency normally required for tenure as associate or full professors on the regular faculty.[16]

Although lacking the total needle count, one would not want to jump too hard on any part of the haystack. The large number of foreign scholars holding tenure at American universities is common knowledge. In the narrow field of Japanese Studies alone, fully 17 percent of the 1,858 individuals listed in the Japan Foundation's 1995 directory of Japan specialists in the United States and Canada were men and women born in Japan.[17] Of the 1,842 specialists giving their present nationality, nearly 13 percent were scholars retaining Japanese citizenship, and of this group 96 held the normally tenured rank of full or associate professor.

To take the echelon of associate and full professors at only two medium-size, medium-ranked campuses on opposite flanks of the nation, the *Guide to Japanese Studies* at the University of Hawaii for 1993–1995 shows a total of seven professors with Japanese surnames (or maiden names) with their undergraduate degrees from Japanese universities among a total of 38 Japan Studies scholars, or almost one in five. Estimating foreign origin more broadly by surnames and provenance of the B.A./B.S. degree, the 1995–1996 undergraduate catalogue of The George Washington University in the nation's capital lists 68 such persons (including but not limited to Australians, Egyptians, Germans, Indians, Peruvians, Rumanians, and Taiwanese) as associate and full professors or research professors—two more tenured foreign faculty members than the entire number at Japan's national universities! If GWU's 76 non-tenured foreign "professorial lecturers," instructors, and assistant, adjunct, and visiting professsors are included, the foreign total rises to 144 or 11.5 percent of an overall faculty of 1,242. Multiply these foreign-tenure statistics by only the top ten of America's heavily internationalized world-class institutions like Berkeley or Harvard, and you already have a Yankee elephant towering over the Nipponese mouse, even allowing for a U.S. population base twice the size of Japan's.[18]

Even more to the point, of course, are the many Japanese nationals to be found in foreign universities teaching mainline disciplines unrelated to Japanese language or culture. These scholars have been able to enter, compete for tenured positions, and win fame at American, European, and Commonwealth universities with no limitation beyond that of their own effort and ability—all while retaining their Japanese citizenship. These have included Susumu Tonegawa at MIT, a Nobel Prize winner in molecular biology; Akira Iriye at Harvard, a past president of the American Historical Association; the internationally known economist and Japanese TV guru Michio Morishima who held a professorship at the London School of Economics from 1970 to 1988; and Hisashi Kobayashi, a recent dean of the prestigious engineering department at Princeton.

Princeton, my own undergraduate alma mater (with a current undergraduate population of approximately 4,500), had on its campus as of April 1993 over 900 foreign students and some 300 foreign faculty members and researchers.[19] This contrasted with a name-brand campus of double Princeton's size in Japan where I once taught. At Gakushuin University— the postwar reincarnation of the aristocratic prewar Peers' School and alma mater of the present Emperor and Crown Prince—there was not a single foreign student or full-time foreign teacher to be found at the combined facility housing the Law and Economics Faculties during that same year, 1993. This sparkling white, new twelve-story building served 81 scholars and about 4,000 undergraduates, many of them specializing in subjects like international politics and law, trade, diplomatic history, and cultural relations—and every one of them was Japanese.

THE LONG ATTITUDINAL SHADOW OF MEIJI

The stubborn strength of Japan's academic apartheid lies deeply embedded in the history and psychology of modern Japan and it will not vanish at a mere wave of the *kokusaika* wand. To understand its persistence we need to look, first, at its original ideological justification and the snail's pace of recently attempted reform.

During the first two decades of the Meiji period (1868–1912) American and European scholars played a founding role in the development of Tokyo University—until 1898 Japan's sole officially recognized "university" and designated as "Imperial" from 1886 through World War II. The earliest wave of foreign teachers was appointed to the highest professorial posts, handsomely remunerated, taught in their own languages, and often doubled as technical advisors to government ministries. They brought the entire corpus of modern Western higher education and learning to Japan at a time when the Japanese had neither the trained scholars nor the translated texts to do so by themselves. By the early 1890s, however, Tokyo Imperial University was ready to "indigenize" (as we would put it today), and when the doors closed in 1893 they did so abruptly and, some foreign observers thought, without sufficient grace.[20]

The operative rationale at the time was best captured in a

reminiscence by Tetsujiro Inoue, first holder of the new German-style professorial chair (*Lehrstuhl*) in philosophy at Tokyo University from 1890 and for some years Dean of the Faculty of Letters (Bungakubu):

> We had many foreigners as teachers at Tokyo University in the early years of Meiji, in order to make up the deficiency in Japanese professors. In principle, however, professors at Japanese universities should all be Japanese. Accordingly, we managed to dismiss the foreign instructors relatively quickly from the Faculties of Medicine, Law, and Science so that there was not one of them left. That was the policy throughout the university. In the Faculty of Letters, too, we were guided by the belief that every field should be taught exclusively by Japanese staff, and that the number of foreigners should gradually be reduced and ultimately eliminated altogether. . . . The Japanese university is a place where Japanese should perform the professorial tasks—it is very different from a colonial university.[21]

In order to maintain a trickle of essential foreign instructors in foreign languages and at posts for which the Japanese were still in training, the Ministry of Education's new ordinance of 1893 established that *gaikokujin kyoshi* category for foreign scholars at national universities, which has continued virtually unchanged into the 1990s.

The ordinance of 1893 in its time may be viewed as a rational step toward self-directed, noncolonial, educational modernization. But the 1880s also happened to be a period marred by reactionary nationalism and emotional antiforeignism. A century later, this "foreign pedagogue" system is a relic of the mid-Meiji period with its forced marches toward modernization, its paranoia toward the Western powers, its wounded national pride under the Unequal Treaties they had imposed, and its desire to absorb the maximum of Western technological expertise with a minimum of outside cultural contamination.

Tokyo Imperial, however, was hardly in danger of becoming another Calcutta University, churning out clerks for a colonial overlord. The Meiji Japanese were in full control of their own educational and intellectual development, and borrowing from the West had been undertaken very consciously in the national interest. Foreign professors and advisors had all been invited over on Japan's terms, and hardly ferried in at gunpoint—although that is how some Japanese at the time apparently viewed them. The Japanese were also in full strategic command of their own territory, with growing military forces sufficient to overwhelm first China and then Russia in 1895 and 1905—during those very years when their schools were nervously banging their doors shut against outsiders. Indeed, from 1893 to the onset of the era of militarism and ultranationalism in 1934, the number of foreign *kyoshi* at Japanese national universities in any given year was usually well under 30, peaking at 41 in 1926—hardly an invading colonial army.[22]

The first wobble forward in new methods for employing foreign scholars came with the passage of the new Kyoin Law of 1982. In the 1970s, as Japan surged toward economic superpower status, the outside world began to take notice of its academic exclusionism. In November 1971, an OECD survey team turned in a rather severe report on its recent visit, noting the closed nature of Japanese university life and the "need for new attitudes." It called on the country to reorient its higher education for "world participation" and "for world needs, not only for Japan's domestic needs," and recommended that the system for employing foreign scholars be entirely revamped to engage them for permanent positions on the same terms as the Japanese.[23]

As with other sectors on Japan's "liberalization" front, the first complaints about the academic closed shop had come from outside the country—yet another example of *gaiatsu* (foreign pressure) having to provide the initial jolt. In an all too familiar sequence, the first response to these pressures came not from the sector to which they had been addressed, but from the political arm. Action would have to be taken, but less on the intrinsic merits of the issue (such as the possible benefits to Japanese education) than to stave off a potentially negative impact on Japan's external relations. Finally the concerned sector—in this case the universities—did what it could to water down the measures about to be foisted on it.

Early pressure for fully tenured teaching positions also came from the resident-Korean academics in Japan. Those with North Korean ties joined hands with the ROK-affiliated in what was part of a wider struggle by Japan's 600,000-strong Korean community to overcome second-class status in the land they had chosen to live in permanently. The Foreign Ministry and the more liberal-minded elements in the Diet and Mon- busho—all concerned over the foreign-policy implications— found themselves pitted against educational nationalists, political conservatives, the Justice Ministry, and the Cabinet Legislation Bureau. The latter stuck by its old legalistic interpre- tation—a pure expression of the old Meiji statism, many Japanese wryly noted—arguing that Japanese citizenship was required of national university professors, "since they are civil servants, and as such participate in the formation of the national will and in the exercise of public power."[24]

This was a dizzily high view of the political impact of routine academic duties. Accordingly, the prohibitions on foreign staff attending and voting at faculty meetings were swept away by the new bill, along with the somewhat higher salaries and all other incongruities save two. *Gaikokujin kyoin* —the new category of "foreign staffers" introduced by the new law—could not be made deans or presidents, but, since these chiefs spent most of their time on budgetary battlefields, this arguably was not the most important test of full collegiality in scholarship and teaching. The matter of tenure, on the other hand, most surely was. The new Kyoin Law as finally passed retreated to a position that allowed the universities to set or not set term limits on foreign appoint- ments as they saw fit, thereby replacing the bolted portal of the closed shop with a revolving door.

At the eleventh hour in the Diet's deliberations, Takeo Nishioka and other members of the ruling party's nationalistic right wing insisted on fixed terms for the new foreign *kyoin*. This, they hoped, would pave the way for similar term-limited con- tracts for the entire Japanese professoriate—a long-sought-for handle on the legion of bothersome left-wing academics. Although there were already numerous devices at hand for tem- porary appointments, conservative politicians argued that inter- national academic exchanges were built around specific short-term projects and that term limitations and a "rotation system" would "facilitate" the foreign hiring process. When the parliamentary committee visited Kyoto University for an academic opinion, President Toshio Sawada (an irrigation engineer) was said to have supported the fixed-term system on the grounds that foreigners preferred specificity in contracts, that the option to "reappoint" gave the system a desirable "flexibility," and that there was considerable anxiety over the qualifications and "compatibility" of scholars hired from other countries.[25] No need to inundate *his* ricefields with the foreign tide.

With much media fanfare, Kyoto University in 1983 hired on three-year contract as full professor a British molecular engineer from Nottingham University who was 58, exactly three years short of Kyoto's mandatory retirement age. By decreeing a three-year term for foreign *kyoin* Kyoto set a mischievous precedent. Only Tokyo University, whose scholars lean heavily on the hospitality of elite schools abroad, made an honest effort to implement the option for open-ended, Japanese-style appointments. Two Americans were hired on a tenure basis in the mid-1980s—an associate professor of geophysics, and a Harvard-trained Taiwanese-American as professor of Chinese Law. Both men were at home in the language and social customs of Japan, lecturing in Japanese to their students and taking full part in departmental meetings and other professional activities.

Oddly enough, even such "native" competence could be, and was, negatively viewed. There was at that time only a minority of scholars at Japan's leading university who insisted that such fluency should be required for permanent appointments of non-Japanese. If that was too much to ask at the time of hiring, then at least as a long-term commitment. That is what Japanese scholars do as a matter of course when they choose to work in the West, and its feasibility in reverse has been richly demonstrated by the foreign missionary staffs at church-affiliated universities throughout East Asia. But the majority at Tokyo University still thought that "internationalization" meant having pure and unacclimated aliens on campus—the two-dimensional presence of the linguistically incapacitated, culture-shocked foreign newcomer as exotic ambience. Or, to use the lament most frequently heard from the foreign teachers themselves: "like pandas at a zoo."

THEY NEVER WILL BE MISSED

From the original introduction of the life-tenured chair or *Lehrstuhl* by German universities in the nineteenth century, to its Japanese adaptation in the national university *koza*, to America's "tenure-track" system, there has been nearly universal recognition that excellence in scholarship and the free expression of ideas are best guaranteed by a settled work environment secure from political harrassment and financial insecurity.

Japanese apologists for the fixed-term system for foreigners have stressed the possibility (at some of the national universities) of open-ended renewals. But the corrosive effect of repeated renewals on a serious scholarly career—and the disingenuousness of equating the possibility of serial reappointments with genuine tenure—were poignantly illustrated by the case of an American friend of mine who survived three rounds of renewals in the 1980s only to be thrown out at the fourth assize.

This scholar, well into his forties at the time, had taught for twelve years in a substantive, non-language discipline at a well-known national university that had been employing him as an "integrated" *kyoin*—under the *new* system—on annual contracts with a triennial review. Although his Japanese was functional and he had done his employers a singular service by launching a record number of seniors into leading graduate schools abroad, he waited anxiously every third year as his name went back into the hopper with all the new prospects both foreign and Japanese. After each reappointment he could look forward to about two years of stabilized work, but from the third he was compelled to start negotiating all over again with the Japanese staff, wondering where a negative verdict might leave him a year later. In the end, he was left on the street, having been ousted to make room for a young protégé of one of his Japanese colleagues. His supporters, originally a majority, took the face-saving exit of abstaining during the vote. "A decade is long enough to have to have taken care of a foreigner," one of the expellers is reported to have exclaimed, as if having permitted a foreigner to work with them for that length of time was a special favor. After stumbling his way through a period of unemployment with three children in school, my friend once again sweats out triennial renewals as *kyoin* at a far less prestigious national university.

An ominous precedent for the multiple foreign staff dismissals of the mid-1990s was set a decade earlier at the brand-new National University of Tsukuba, located in the flat sedgy marshlands of ex-urban Ibaraki Prefecture, an hour's train ride north of Tokyo. Tsukuba was created during the 1970s with hefty political and financial support from the ruling party, the business establishment, and the national treasury to serve as Japan's "new-model," path-breaking university for the "age of internationalization." In April 1985—after the start of the new academic year, and with no place for them to go—the university summarily fired, as a result of its own internal politics, four of its longer-serving *kyoshi*, who had already been asked not to move elsewhere and promised a new five-year contract period as Tsukuba's first *kyoin* starting that month.

The Korean historian Dr. Dong Jin Kang and Dr. Margarete Sawada, a political scientist from West Germany whose Japanese husband also taught at Tsukuba, were *kyoshi* of professorial-equivalent rank who had been at Tsukuba for seven years when the trouble started. Junior to them were Dr. Nicholas Teele, an American specialist in Chinese and Japanese classical literature who had previously served as a Fulbright professor in Seoul, and a young Taiwanese instructor in Chinese language, Liang-tse Chang. In 1984, all four had agreed in writing to relinquish their *kyoshi* posts as of 1985, since Tsukuba had recently introduced a four-year cut-off for that category. All four, however, had been officially graded and approved for transfer to the new *kyoin* status and were asked to sit tight while their prospective reappointments were steered through the shoals of academic politics and the brewing storm of a bitterly contested presidential election.

After waiting out an anxious year, all four found themselves suddenly unemployed months too late for applying to other universities. Kang took the university to court, but died a broken man just days before the main hearing. As a *kyoshi* myself at

Tsukuba's College of International Relations from 1984 to1987
I watched these academic iniquities sympathetically from a safe
distance, and was happy to leave Tsukuba's rurally isolated, for-
eigner-unfriendly campus of my own volition for a visiting professorship at Keio, set amid the urban amenities of Tokyo. I
never met Dr. Kang, but his predicament was the archetype of
what many others have since experienced, and the brief tale that
follows is in part my personal tribute to the memory of an
immensely courageous man whose lonely fight against Japan's
academic apartheid may, quite literally, have cost him his life.

A Korean Confronts His Tormentors

Seven years at Tsukuba, Dong Jin Kang had smelled a rat
from the very start. Probing and recording every move that the
university made in his direction, he ended up with a twelve-
page handwritten chronicle of promises made and broken.[26]

The dismissal of this South Korean historian, 59 years of age at
the time, was doubly poignant in that he was one of the first foreigners to have received a doctoral degree from Japan's premier
school, Tokyo University. Considering the reverence in which the
Japanese hold their own first graduates from places like the
Harvard Law School or Oxbridge, one would have expected a
more protective—if indeed not celebrative—attitude toward him.

Unlike the Japan-born Korean scholars, Dr. Kang was graduated from the Law Faculty of Seoul National University—the
Republic of Korea's equivalent of Tokyo, the very top of the
deck—and had held a professorship at a private university in
his own country before coming to Japan for his doctorate. A
specialist on Korean-Japanese relations, he had been giving
courses and seminars in Korean, Japanese, and East Asian
history in the Humanities College, the East Asia masters'
program, and the doctoral program in history and anthropology. The author of over ten books and more than a hundred
articles, Kang may not have been a Toynbee or a Levi-Strauss—
and who in the name of heaven was, at Tsukuba?—but he was
by all accounts a first-rate scholar of whom any first-rate university could justly be proud.

With a variety of blandishments, Dean Shinpei Kato of the

Humanities College urged Dr. Kang to sign his waiver in late 1983.

"It won't apply to scholars with substantial achievements. . . . It's a mere formality. We can't ask only those [whom we'd like to get rid of] to sign it, so we're getting signatures from everybody. That's all there is to it."

"Well, have those to whom it does apply sign it," Kang replied, refusing to comply. "I have no need to do so."

A week later, Kato was back, claiming to speak this time for Professor Tadashi Sato of the Planning Office. "We're giving you a *kyoin* position year after next, so don't leave for another school," he announced. "Please don't mention it to the other foreign *kyoshi*. . . . But if you don't sign the waiver we can't even give you a contract this coming year."

Shinpei Kato, an anthropologist, seemed quite sure of the matter, but Kang still demurred. "Other places have approached me," he replied. "In a matter as weighty as this I must have clear assurances."

Dr. Kang claimed also to have been promised a transfer to the *kyoin* rolls by Professor Noboru Haga, chairman of the Institute of History and Anthropology—the research echelon to which he would be attached if given the new position. At Tsukuba, the institutes provide a scholar's primary affiliation and identity. Assignment to one of the teaching colleges, i.e., departments, for classroom duties comes later. The foreign *kyoshi*, in yet another downgrading of academic status, are kept out of the research institutes and assigned by the central administration directly to the colleges.

The encouragement from fellow historian Haga therefore carried considerable weight in Kang's mind. Haga also urged him to trust Dean Kato, noting that he was a member of the personnel committee. The Korean scholar realized that he now had strongly expressed commitments from the three persons who would be most influential in securing his new appointment—his prospective institute chief, his college dean, and the planning office head. He concluded that, with that sort of backing, it would be rude on his part to delay any further. Reluctantly, then, on 30 March 1984—the penultimate day of the 1983 academic year—Kang signed his waiver.

November 1984 rolled around with no forward movement on the promised post for 1985. Seeking particulars from Dean Kato, Kang was told, "We are all working on it, so please wait." Subsequent queries brought the same response, so he had reason to believe that all was going well. His expectations were reinforced when he learned that the professors at the Institute of History and Anthropology had voted unanimously to accept him as a member, and that as early as July the humanities dean had forwarded to the administration's faculty personnel committee the preliminary documents for his "tenure" appointment.

At the turn of the year, the mood was still upbeat among Dr. Kang's friends and other Japanese staff sympathetic to the four foreigners, since so much had been promised so openly by so many to so few.

It was not as though MacArthur was landing once again. There were, after all, only four barbarian intruders under consideration for joining a Japanese faculty of over 3,800. Tsukuba had a three-notch yardstick for evaluating foreign *kyoshi*. An "A" ranking specifically indicated a standard suitable for appointment as *kyoin*, and all four had passed that test. "Even the president guarantees the four foreigners," Professor Haga told Kang in early January. "Just let me handle it . . . just wait a little longer."

But around 20 February 1985, things came unstuck, the buck-passing began, and the record starts to read more and more like a typical Japan-U.S. trade negotiation.

Checking with humanities Dean Kato that day to see how things stood—a bare five weeks before the new school year—Dr. Kang was told that his new appointment was in trouble, that Kato's own leverage had reached its limit, and that he should seek the help of institute chairman Haga, who had more authority. This time Haga was all high-handedness when Kang approached him. "Since you signed the waiver, the university has no more public answerability towards you," he flung back in cold anger. "If you have some other place you can go to, try going there even now. . . . You and (Mrs.) Sawada are floating in the air. . . . And don't try seeing the president, it will only make things worse. . . . I am the one who is going to make the final decision on this," Haga ranted on, according to Kang's published testimony.

A subsequent investigation into the matter by the Vice President for Research Development, Junnosuke Nakai, who was also Chairman of the Faculty Personnel Committee, revealed that the recommending papers for Dr. Kang from the humanities college had never reached the committee. Indeed, they had never been forwarded.

Meeting Kang shortly thereafter, Dean Kato explained that the Vice President for Administration, Etsuyuki Matsuura, had quashed the recommendation and that the file still sat on his own desk. "I'm sorry, I've been telling you lies all along," Kato lamely apologized. "But now, under instructions from the personnel committee chief, I'm planning to submit the papers once again . . . and if they pass this time, you'll be a regular professor just like me." At the same time Kang heard it from a colleague that Professor Haga—recently elevated to Vice President for Student Affairs—had passed word to the effect that, "It will take a little time since we have to prepare fresh documents, but I intend without fail to do my best for Dr. Kang."

But Kang no longer believed it. They had been planning all along to consign him to oblivion. He had begun to see through it and concluded that all their recent moves were simply tricks to stay ahead of him.

Engaging a lawyer, he submitted to the administration a petition with full particulars of what had happened. He received no reply. Requesting a meeting with university officials, he failed to get that either. After dogged persistence, making repeated demands and allowing that he would not rule out taking legal action, Kang was finally granted a brief meeting, around noon on commencement day in the last week of March 1985 with Personnel Chairman Nakai and Vice President Matsuura—reputedly the most powerful man in the daily running of the campus. Kang used the meeting to detail the lengthy indignity to which he had been subjected. He had been pushed to the limits of his physical and mental endurance. He therefore requested the immediate honoring of their promises.

"We have absolutely no intention of driving you out of the university or doing anything like that," Matsuura assured him. "How could we simply fire a person whose very livelihood is at stake?" Foisting the blame now on Professor Tadashi Sato, who had recently moved up from the planning office to become Vice President for Academic Affairs, Matsuura delivered himself of an emphatic pledge. "Actually, he's the man who made up all of those new regulations and all that. . . . I'll take up your case when we get into April. . . . Since you have it from the two of us here, you can absolutely count on it. Please set your mind at rest."

Vice President Matsuura, like President Nobuyuki Fukuda, was a physicist—the regal discipline at Tsukuba. Both men had belonged to the powerful, rightish, Monbusho-favored in-group at the now extinct Tokyo University of Education (Kyoikudai), which had been dismantled to create Tsukuba University. In the mid-1970s, over the protest of Kyoikudai's old-fashioned left-wing majority, they had led the move to the new campus. Matsuura explained to Dr. Kang that he had been obliged to pigeonhole his *kyoin* recommendation because it would never do to have recommendations for all those *other* foreign *kyoshi* inundating the personnel committee. Promising to reintroduce Kang's case without fail at the April 5 meeting of the personnel committee, Matsuura once again told the hapless Korean professor not to worry and took his leave on a firm handshake.

For all that, Matsuura failed to bring up Kang's case on the fifth and started beating around the bush in several new directions. He would take it up at the next meeting, he said. Things were not going smoothly because there was some other person who had been defaming Kang. Even without the new position he would see to it that the university gave Kang a decent salary.

Professor Nakai, too, had gone into reverse gear, arguing that promises from high officials in the administration had been "mere private mutterings" and held no weight with him as personnel committee chief.

Realizing that all the promises and fabrications had been no more than stratagems to gain time, Kang took Tsukuba University—technically speaking, the Japanese state—to court. Securing a temporary restraining order to uphold his current status, he instituted a suit for reinstatement at the district court in Mito. The preliminary hearing was held in October 1985, but litigation was expected to drag out two years to final verdict.

"There was not a shred of sincerity in the administration's

attitude toward me," Dr. Kang told the student newspaper. "Here's somebody who's eating out of the same rice bowl with them, but instead of trying to solve problems in a friendly manner, they have consistently dealt with me—I regret to say—from a posture of hostility and through deceitful methods."

And to the *Asahi Jaanaru* (Asahi Journal) he summed it all up: "These iniquitous, secretive personnel actions have been hatched in a hothouse—the direct outcome of the high-handedness, bureaucratism, and abnormally anti-internationalist disposition of Tsukuba's top executives. The criterion for tenuring foreign *kyoshi* has been based not on scholarly work or on ability as an educator or a researcher, but on personal pull and sycophancy. . . . They don't think of the foreign *kyoshi* as human beings, an attitude that flies in the face of international trust and the spirit of the new law."

The court order guaranteed Kang his base salary and the continued use of his office, faculty housing, and university medical services. No longer, however, could he appear before his students in the classroom. Indeed, in all of this no thought had been given to the needs of the students or the well-being of the curriculum. Most of the courses scheduled for Drs. Kang and Sawada in 1985 went untaught, or they were picked up by temporaries or by colleagues with very different interests later on in the year or in 1986—being given under the same formal title but with greatly altered content. Several graduate students were left dangling without their thesis adviser, and were arbitrarily assigned to other scholars.

Drs. Kang, Sawada, and Teele all came to believe that they were victims of back-alley jockeying for position preliminary to the presidential election scheduled for March 1986 when the incumbent, Fukuda, would complete his final term. The acknowledged front-runner, Vice President Matsuura—so the prevailing theory went—had been given a scare by Vice President Tadashi Sato's good showing in the previous contest, so he had set out to undermine Sato and all his works, including his plan to rehire the four foreign *kyoshi* in new *kyoin* posts. Matsuura apparently engineered the barring of Sato from reelection as vice-president while the latter was temporarily immobilized in a hospital, and he came to take an increasingly hard antiforeign line as part of his own campaign platform.

Looking beyond his own personal plight, Kang regretted that so much was going on that had no bearing on the proper business of a center of higher learning. "They're treating this university as though it's their private property!" he fumed. "If they had even a scrap of concern for the education of the students, or for international trust in their handling of the foreign *kyoshi*, none of this could have happened."

But Kang's agony was far from over. Brimming with vigorous fighting spirit during the first year, 1986 found him bedridden at the university hospital with a life-threatening ailment that was slipping in and out of remission. (Much later, in 1993, a distinguished Korean historian in Seoul, a former president of the Korean Historical Association, told me that the entire Korean academic community knew of the incident at Tsukuba. Kang, I learned, had always been a physically powerful man, a mountain climber who had earned money in his student days by working as a day laborer on a spare diet of Chinese noodles.)

On 6 October 1986, the *Asahi Shinbun* reported that Dr. Kang had withdrawn his suit on 30 September after being told by university representatives that they would take "favorable action"—unspecified at the time—if he did so. On the sixth Tsukuba announced that it was reappointing him as a visiting professor. The *Asahi* described the development as an "amicable settlement," a result of the new president's determination to reform his fractious administration. Professor Koichi Anan— a gentle, unassuming, and thoroughly unpolitical biochemist and former head of the Medical School—had been elected by a last-minute rallying of anti-Matsuura forces. "We welcome the withdrawal of the suit. The appointment as visiting professor is a tribute to Dr. Kang's scholarly achievements," a university spokesman purred.

Alas, poor Kang should have known better—and also the *Asahi*, with its longstanding distrust of the Tsukuba establishment. Three days later, on 9 October, the newspaper returned to the story with more detail and concluded that Kang's professional situation was still far from stable. Friends of his at Tsukuba painted an even grimmer picture. As Kang's health declined so had his bargaining position with the university. And, as he came to suspect that the end was near, he may have become increasingly anxious for any settlement that would redeem his honor and mark a victory of sorts in his long struggle with the university. Once again, however, Tsukuba deceived him.

The visiting professorship turned out to be a purely honorific title, intended only for research, and with no money attached to it. This was a rarely used category that had been conjured up to accommodate visiting researchers, foreigners for the most part, whose salaries were being paid by their home universities or governments. To generate a semblance of income, and to provide a teaching slot for the course on historical documents that Kang had been offered by his old humanities college, Tsukuba had simultaneously appointed him to a part-time lectureship. Being in the hospital most of the time, Kang was unable to avail himself even of this pittance of a salary. And there was the grand clincher—both appointments were to run only until March 1987, the end of the current academic year, then a mere five months away.

Kang had withdrawn his suit for a mess of pottage less than a week before it was due for the main trial at Mito. Extensive depositions prepared by Professor T. Sato, the German Dr. Sawada, and other informed parties were thereby lost to the judicial record. Kang's friends told me that the negotiating position of the university's representatives had gone up and down with the medical prognoses for his condition.

"This is not the professorship or associate professorship I had been hoping for, but this is one step forward toward that final goal, and I expect all the more favorable action to be taken from now," Dr. Kang told the *Asahi*. His lawyer echoed the same hope, but in the paper's judgment there really was no firm prospect for him for the next academic year starting April 1987. Asked about that, Vice President Fumihiko Takano told the *Asahi*, "We can't tell until that time. We'll just have to wait and see."

The term "favorable action" used by both Kang and the university in this contretemps is one destined to bring a sardonic chuckle from old U.S. trade negotiators. *Zensho suru* is the phrase that Prime Minister Eisaku Sato employed in December 1969 to reassure President Richard Nixon that, in return for the agreed-upon reversion of Okinawa, he would "take favorable action" to curb the Japanese textile exports that were burning a hole in the president's Southern electoral strategy. When the textiles continued their unabated flow, and Nixon realized he had bought a pig in a poke, he returned the favor in July 1971 by pointedly failing to inform Japan when he suddenly opened talks with China and sent the dollar plunging in a free float.

Zensho suru is not one of those unequivocal Japanese euphemisms whereby everybody knows that the "yes" just uttered really means "no." It is a genuinely ambivalent and obfuscating expression, whence its great popularity. Its literal meaning is, precisely, "to take favorable action"—the sense in which Kang was using it, and in which the university obviously intended him to understand it. Its practical nuance, however, leaves the judgment of what is "favorable" to the discretion of the party being asked to do something—not to the person requesting. "Leave it to me, I'll deal with it wisely," or, simply, "I'll do my best," better reflect the actual level of commitment.

Very shortly thereafter Dr. Kang died at the Tsukuba University Hospital at the age of 61. The university, however, was not above visiting one final indignity upon his wife and son before they bore his ashes home. As his widow was clearing out their apartment in the foreign faculty residence, the administration dunned her for payment of over one million yen in back rent.

Although Kang had continued to occupy these quarters under the terms of the court order, his *gaikokujin kyoshi* housing allowance had been suspended. I heard from my own departmental chairman at Tsukuba that the university had kept in reserve a considerable sum of money for back salary, as well as an old *kyoshi* slot, in the event Kang had won his suit. Instead, with the "troublemaker" gone, Tsukuba pounced on his heirs.

Kang had been a poor man, and the bill was well beyond his widow's means. Some friends proposed a campaign to raise these funds on campus, but others objected, fearing that certain scholars and students might use the issue to embarrass the university in public. Others suggested she simply pack up and go, assuring her that the university could then—with no real bother to itself—write off the loss as an "abandonment of premises, tenant absconding." Mrs. Kang rejected the suggestion.

To the bitter end, Tsukuba showed itself more concerned with form than with substance. No matter what the affront to common sense or simple human decency, it was okay so long as the files were in order.

No Protest: The Academic Samurai as Wimp

The more profound implications of this story lie in the lack of response by Tsukuba's scholars and Japan's educational leaders. By no rational yardstick was the case of the four foreign scholars incidental. If Japan truly intended to lower the human tariff barrier in higher education, here was an opportunity with more of the necessary ingredients in place than ever before—a new campus officially dedicated to openness, a new law removing all the formal barriers, and a crop of seasoned candidates already stamped "Grade A."

The summary dismissal of these foreigners was carried out in a fashion that would have evoked passionate protest among colleagues and cries of racial prejudice had it happened to Japanese staff on an American campus. One can easily imagine the storm of indignation in Japan's mass media, the anxious investigations by Japanese consular officials, the breast-beating and *mea culpa* in the American press.

Indeed, something very much like that occurred in 1987—over a temporary visitor, no long-standing colleague—when the University of Rochester, to protect a new technology, refused to accept into one of its seminars an employee of a Japanese competitor of Eastman Kodak, the sponsor of the program. Responding to the public uproar this provoked, Rochester agreed to admit the visitor, but by then he had been received into the consoling bosom of MIT.

In the case of Tsukuba's foreign professors, neither the Japanese staff—many of whom had received their higher degrees or taught at American campuses—nor the great national pundits of "internationalization" and "mutual understanding" raised their voices over this scandal. The entire machinery of Japan's educational, press, and cultural-exchange establishment chose to ignore it, with the single exception of the liberal-left leaning *Asahi*, which for years had been monitoring what it viewed as

Tsukuba's drift toward rightish nationalism and bureaucratic heavy-handedness. Japan's second largest daily newspaper also continued to expose the university's covert promotion of student and professorial elements with ties to the Unification Church movement of the Reverend Sun Myung Moon—at a campus officially dedicated to political neutrality and a fresh break with Japan's debilitating left-right ideological confrontations.

There was a delicious irony in Tsukuba's protestation that it had made no written commitments to the four foreigners. For years, in business negotiations and cultural forums, Japanese have twitted Westerners over their fixation on scraps of paper and their overreliance on formal contractual undertakings. American salesmen who leave Tokyo convinced they have a deal simply because they have someone's signature on a document have often come a cropper. In Japan—so goes the avuncular advice—what really counts is personal trust, the fine nuancing of spoken words, that meaningful look in the eye. These, of course, were precisely what the four *kyoshi* had been banking on when they signed their waivers and swallowed the hook of prospective *kyoin* appointments, which had been baited with personal importunings, verbal undertakings, and reassuring glances, grunts, and nods.

As Dr. Margarete Sawada remarked to the student newspaper, "The Japanese are of the opinion that, while oral promises have binding force among Japanese, Westerners will not consider as binding anything that is not committed to writing in fine detail. That is a misconception. In the West, too, we are bound to honor verbal pledges."

More telling than the university's legal arguments, however, were some of the rebuttals that high Tsukuba officials essayed in response to outside criticism. In 1978 the then Vice President Fukuda, in support of the proposed new Kyoin Law, had marvelled that "even" Nobel Prize–winning foreigners could not receive tenured positions in Japan. By 1985 President Nobuyuki Fukuda's personnel committee chief was reported as having proclaimed that it was Tsukuba's intention to engage as permanent staff "only" such foreign scholars as had won, or been candidates for, the Nobel Prize. "Why do we need to have foreigners teach things that Japanese are capable of handling?" he added.[27] Here was a pure emanation of the philosophy of the Meiji government a century earlier. Foreign scholars, it seemed, were still but temporary transmitters of knowledge, to be celebrated, sucked dry, and sacked.

Writing in Japan's venerable intellectual monthly, *Chuo Koron*, Dr. Sawada asked how the Nobel yardstick would work if applied even-handedly to Tsukuba's Japanese and foreign staff. "Of the [Japanese] teaching staff of 79 in the College of Comparative Culture, only 20 percent hold the Ph.D., and 17 percent of the full professors have only a B.A. In contrast to that, about 30 percent of Tsukuba's 31 foreign *kyoshi* have their doctorates." Did anyone seriously suppose that Nobel-caliber academics would come to take up *kyoin* positions that were limited to five years? The university already had a visiting scholar category to accommodate those super-scholars who, if they came at all, would want to stay at the most one or two years. The new law had been written, Dr. Sawada emphasized, to link Japanese universities more closely to the outside world by opening up Japan's permanent academic job market. And what would happen if Japan's ethnocentric principle were applied to Japanese now teaching abroad? "Except for instructors in the Japanese language," she drove home, "they would all have to be fired."[28]

Britain's *Nature* magazine criticized Tsukuba in a lengthy story and editorial in October 1985:

> The rule limiting employment [for kyoshi] to four years is seen as particularly repressive. Its justification is that it is better to have a large number of different teachers than a few who stay a long time. But if that is true why not insist all staff—Japanese and foreign alike—are replaced every four years? Clearly the policy would be disastrous. The rule only makes sense to someone who sees foreigners as different species from the Japanese; not to be treated as equal and responsible members of the university staff.[29]

I could only marvel at the see-no-evil/hear-no-evil/speak-no-evil response of Tsukuba staff who had benefitted from long years of training, teaching, or even tenured employment in the U.S. and other foreign countries. The sole exception was one of the university's highest officials who was elected to his post after the incident had already been swept under the rug. Penning his thoughts by hand in shaky English on ordinary stationery paper, invariably mailed privately from his own home to mine, this gentleman conveyed a quiet personal warmth and a troubled conscience over the turn things had taken. By then I had deplored the Tsukuba incident in a leading Japanese educational journal,[30] and he sought my understanding for the enormous leverage held by the Monbusho over any would-be innovations by Tsukuba's administrators. I was genuinely touched that he wrote at all, but it was a pity he too lacked the courage to make his views public.

QUARANTINING THE VIRUS

This fending off of foreign professors reflects a broader tendency to marginalize foreigners within Japanese organizations that is inversely proportional to their command of the Japanese language and social behavior. Although Japanese constantly complain that foreigners do not make a sufficient effort to master these, it is precisely when the outsider has achieved linguistic and social "fluency" and (for whatever family or professional reasons) makes a career commitment to work *in* Japan that the quarantining psychology comes into play. One suspects that, along with some of Tokyo's more Western-oriented lawyers, Japanese scholars too are loathe to see the authentic and nonmediated voices of physically present foreigners erode their own century-long role and self-image as *the* authorities on the outside world.

The desire for participation and full professional acceptance is, however, only human. After all, what is the point of making that cultural and linguistic investment in the first place? Surely not just to be able to take a more indulgent attitude toward Japan's trade policies—which often seems to be the stunted end-purpose of Japan's "cultural diplomacy." For any person anywhere in the world undertaking to cross a major cultural divide, the quest inevitably develops a personal dimension. Ultimately, one's relationship to a foreign culture has to be grounded in human contact and empathy.

This point was well put by Kazuyuki Kitamura, former head of Japan's premier research center on higher education at Hiroshima University. He draws a distinction between the true integration of tenure and the sort of noisily bruited short-term visitor exchanges that many Japanese universities try to pass off as "*kokusaika.*" Kitamura, who is Japan's foremost advocate of giving tenure to qualified foreigners, argues that the challenge lies in, "welcoming foreigners with a different cultural background and way of thinking as our comrades and professional colleagues," and in admitting them to the "common quest for general learning" and to a "shared community life." Even though the real hitches are attitudinal rather than legal, the central practical question on which it all turns is that of tenured appointments. The matter will not be fundamentally tackled by "the warm reception of foreigners as occasional guests" or by "sprucing up the physical plant for cultural exchange," Kitamura insists.[31] Nor, I would add, by synchronizing school-year calendars, working out equivalencies for academic degrees, getting the Japanese to speak better English, or introducing more foreign area studies into the university curriculum. These are important blocks in the "internationalization" edifice, but not the capstone.

How little Japanese attitudes toward foreign academics have changed over the past hundred years is suggested by the experience of one of the most illustrious of the early *kyoshi*, the Leipzig-trained physician Erwin Baelz, who served from 1876 to 1902 as chief adviser in developing the medical school and hospital at Tokyo University. Dr. Baelz's diary reveals a gradual devolution from his admiration in the 1870s for Japan's eagerness for Western knowledge, to his indignation in the 1880s as he watched growing numbers of foreign colleagues dismissed and repatriated without any thanks for their contributions, to his own frustration in the 1890s as he found himself bypassed in major faculty decisions and sought to leave but was repeatedly held back by unfulfilled promises to improve his situation.

At his own twenty-fifth anniversary festivities in 1901, Baelz touched on what he saw as the root cause of Japan's shabby treatment of foreign scholars. The Japanese, Baelz suggested, often seemed not to understand the true source and nature of Western science, mistaking it for a sort of machine that could be easily carted off to new places and made to perform the same work, rather than seeing it as an organism requiring a carefully nurturing atmosphere. Foreign scholars from many countries had worked hard to implant the spirit of modern science in Japan, but although they had come to nurture the tree itself, their mission had largely been misunderstood. The Japanese had treated them as no more than peddlers of the final fruits, and had been content to take the latest plums from them, without seeking to appropriate the spirit that had nourished the tree. Baelz concluded:

> Soon there will be very few foreign teachers left in the country. Let me advise you to give those that still remain more freedom than you have done in the past, more opportunity for independent work; and let me urge you to keep in close touch with them in fields besides that of their strictly educational work. . . . In that way you will learn more of the spirit of science, the spirit with which you cannot become intimately acquainted in lecture theaters . . . but only in daily association with those engaged in research."[32]

The insular mentality so starkly exposed by the academic cartel of the mind also casts its long shadow on the more transient presence of foreign researchers and students. For these we may stick to the symptoms, having already diagnosed the disease.

4

PASSING PRESENCES
Scientific Researchers and Foreign Students

Although normally in Japan for a brief sojourn, foreign students and scientific researchers encounter a variety of institutional and psychological barriers that shed additional light on that fundamental attitude toward foreign intellectual presences pinpointed by Erwin Baelz a century ago—excessively instrumental, while minimally engaged.

This attitude is best exposed in its personal aspect by the experience of foreign students. Its negative impact on American competitiveness has caused growing pressures by the U.S. for greater access to Japanese laboratories by Americans in science and technology.

RESEARCHERS AND TECHNOLOGICAL ACCESS: THE CUTTING EDGE

"HOW JAPAN PICKS AMERICA'S BRAINS," warned the heavy black headline in the *Fortune* magazine article for 21 December 1987. "Much of its economic success has been built on bought, borrowed, or stolen technology. Now U.S. companies are striking back—but a two-way street is still far off," added the subhead. The author, Joel Dreyfuss, was calling national attention to the starkly unbalanced flow of scientific and technological information between the two countries and the lack of opportunities for American scientific researchers to train, study, work, or find long-term professional positions in the university, government, and corporate laboratories of Japan.

Because this aspect of Japan's intellectual insularism has the most obvious impact on the U.S. national interest and, like the issue of lawyers, involves distinctly economic matters such as patents, Japan's scientific research and its R & D for commercial applications have attracted a great deal of attention from American officials, writers, and scholars. The National Academy of Sciences completed a two-year study of this issue in non-defense-related fields in late 1996, and I thus confine myself here to a quick sketch of Japan's best-explored cartel of the mind.

In 1985, the Nakasone cabinet took a series of initiatives that included an expanded goal for admitting foreign students. In order to overcome Japan's traditional weakness in basic scientific research and to create a world-class science and technology infrastructure that would no longer be dependent on foreign break-throughs, they also called for greater international exchanges with scientists. It is no coincidence that the call came in the mid-1980s at a time when Japan was under unprecedented foreign pressure to dismantle its import and investment barriers. While heralding the imminent arrival of "internationalization" on all fronts, Tokyo actually was very worried that market liberalization, especially in the new information technologies, would preempt Japan's effort to achieve its own indigenous capacity for R & D in cutting-edge hi-tech industries.[1]

At about the same time, American science and technology began to shed some of its lordly postwar ethnocentrism, thanks to which U.S. technology had been licensed to Japanese corporations for minimal benefits in return. For much of the postwar period the growing presence of Japanese researchers and funding in the U.S. had been viewed as no more than a natural, nonproblematical tribute to the superiority of American science. But now a shift in U.S. attitudes reflected an increasing concern about the growing proportion of foreign nationals of all kinds in the American scientific and engineering workforce

from the standpoints of national security, economic competitiveness, and jobs.[2]

Basically there are two ways of acquiring advanced technology from a foreign country: to buy it outright, or to study it
on its home ground. One can also buy access to those study
opportunities, and U.S. concern over Japan now extends to all
three areas—technology flows, access for researchers, and
Japanese money at American universities. On the economic or
heavy end of the stick, Americans have become more careful
about one-sided transfers of their manufacturing technology to
the Japanese through licensing and joint ventures without a
guaranteed reciprocal flow of know-how (such as grant-back
rights on any improvements). This turn was dramatized by the
congressional and Pentagon pressures to renegotiate the terms
for codevelopment of the next-generation FSX fighter plane in
1987. The agenda for the "framework" talks between the two
governments now includes technological access and intellectual
property rights—perhaps the most critical U.S. economic issue
now with all of Asia. And the first half of the 1990s has seen
stepped-up litigation by U.S. corporations against patent viola-
tions by Japanese firms, together with a broader challenge to
Japanese patent laws, and plans to weaken copyright protection
for computer programs by legalizing "decompilation." This
reverse engineering of intellectual property is an issue that also
involves the Cultural Affairs Agency (Bunkacho), a division of
the Japanese Ministry of Education (Monbusho).

Evaluating the human side of the science and technology
imbalance requires a more subjective judgment. U.S. science
officials managing the exchange of personnel with Japan
include not only technonationalist Cassandras but also
Pollyannas of the so-called "global village" school. The latter
view scientific research as an increasingly borderless and interdependent activity under which unreciprocated research opportunities present no particular threat to the national interest. The
United States in any case is not about to disinvite its foreign
researchers. Americans, unlike the Japanese, have always
viewed intellectual ties as a two-way opportunity rather than a
zero-sum game. They recognize that their foreign colleagues
and students, while no doubt picking America's brain in the

process, also contribute their brainpower to our own science and technology agenda and help to make up an important shortfall of U.S. citizens in the lower and less well-paid rungs of scientific teaching and research at American universities and government institutes.

Japan, nevertheless, stands very high in the overall presence of foreigners at American universities, having displaced China in 1994–1995 as the leading source of foreign students, with 45,276 or 10 percent of the total foreign student population of 452,635. Among foreign university teachers and researchers who are not permanent U.S. residents, Japan placed second after China with 5,155 or 8.9 percent of the 58,074 total.[3] Given the relatively low emphasis placed by Japanese corporations on the Ph.D., it is perhaps not surprising that the Japanese came in eleventh among the doctorates awarded to non-U.S. citizens in science and engineering in 1991, a mere 120 out of 8,504.[4] As of early 1996, however, they ranked first with 346 visiting scholars at the National Institutes of Health (NIH)—one of the most sought-after of the government institutes—ahead of the Chinese and the Italians.[5] Quite a number of Japanese researchers at U.S. university laboratories of course come for relatively brief stays on a non-degree basis. Many are sent by Japanese firms or government agencies, some to slots earmarked by Japanese contributions to the respective universities.

One recent set of Japanese statistics for what would be roughly the U.S. 1992–1993 academic year, showed a total of 722 researchers in science and technology dispatched to the U.S. from Japanese companies, national institutes, and universities—a figure 5.9 times the reverse flow. Of the Japanese, 44 were placed with American companies (a ratio of 6.3:1), 87 at U.S. national institutes (6.7:1), and 591 (5.8:1) at universities. Of the 122 Americans traveling the other way, 7 were at Japanese companies, 13 at national institutes, and 102 at Japanese universities. The imbalance with the West as a whole is reduced to a ratio of 3:1, however, when all the advanced nations are included with the United States, reflecting perhaps a more energetic promotion of Japan exchanges by European governments and/or a relative lack of positions at EC laboratories.[6]

The real problem with the imbalance in researchers, however, lies less in raw numbers than in the type and quality of access they enjoy in their host country's research institutions. Japanese, like other foreign scientists, have been able to pursue higher degrees in the U.S., join the regular staff of American academic, government, and corporate laboratories, rise, if they can, to the highest professional positions, and participate in the core work of path-breaking projects before they return—as many of them eventually do—to Japan, taking their expertise with them.

The reverse is not possible for foreigners studying in Japan. And it is not primarily a matter of language. A command of Japanese, while important for long-term professional adjustment and social comfort, has probably been exaggerated as an "American barrier" to enhanced exchange. For example, Tokyo University's doctoral programs in science and technology for foreigners are now conducted primarily in English, and given the fact that so many Japanese scientists have trained abroad, language *per se* is not that much of a functional handicap in laboratory work.

The most direct tapping of the American brain, of course, is carried out by Japanese corporations that have invested in various devices for research access in the United States. There are for starters the old, unexceptionably capitalist, expedients of funding contract research or buying into America's small start-up companies with a promising edge in hi-tech. Japanese corporations have also established their own R & D facilities— freestanding entities, as opposed to in-house research departments—in the U.S., with functions that include the monitoring and acquisition of American technology. As of 1992 over half of such foreign-owned research facilities in the U.S., 155 out of 255, were Japanese, smaller in scale but more numerous than their European counterparts. By way of contrast, there were 71 U.S.-operated R & D facilities in Japan in 1990 (40 of them wholly American owned), mainly engaged in new-product development.[7] Many of the Japanese-owned laboratories in the U.S. are located close to America's major research universities, such as the NEC Research Institute and NEC Open Systems Lab at Princeton, where they offer consultancies to faculty members, internships to students, and jobs to freshly minted Ph.D.s.

The most worrisome aspect of Japan's funding of American research is its invasion of the internal structure and ethos of the university itself. Grants, subventions, and endowments are sometimes given with substantial strings attached—be they a specific line of research or access to research results or project participation for personnel dispatched by the Japanese donor. Japan's largesse has also been showered, of course, on nonscientific fields like Japanese Studies, but the worry there has been—crudely put—less over nibbling at America's brain for benefits to Japanese industry than about stuffing it with approved images of Japan.

The sheer scale of Tokyo's science and technology investment in American academe is suggested by the single case of the Massachusetts Institute of Technology, which has 14 Japan-endowed professorial chairs. In 1989, Kyocera donated $1 million for a chair in ceramics. In 1990, a banner year, MIT took in from Japan $10 million from the Ministry of International Trade and Industry (MITI) for rights to use the Media Laboratory; $3 million over five years from Nintendo for a study at the same laboratory of how children learn while at play; and $3 million from Nippon Telegraph and Telephone Data Communications over 1989–1991 to help establish the computer center for the Institute of Intelligence Technology Engineering System Laboratory.[8]

It is only fair to add, of course, that the American universities have actively solicited these contributions, and that the Japanese for their part have not hesitated to shut the purse on very large requests when they sensed they would be kept on the periphery, as with the U.S. government's failed Superconducting Super Collider (SSC) project in 1991. Be that as it may, the nub of the matter is that a receptivity by Japanese academe to similarly tied science and technology funding from the United States is simply inconceivable. The very thought of it would be laughed out of court.

In the technology race with Tokyo, Americans understandably have been more concerned with big-ticket hardware issues like semiconductors, or the large number of Japanese researchers on their own campuses. But the obstacles their own scientists and engineers have encountered in Japan, with respect to research activities and access, parallel those faced by other foreign professionals. These barriers, if allowed to stand, may prove to be the most detrimental to the United States in macroeconomic terms over the long run.

There are, to begin with, important differences between the two countries' systems for research as well as in their attitudes toward access to information—the latter even more pronounced than in the case of the journalists. Essentially, the United States since World War II has concentrated on basic research and defense-related R & D at the expense of commercial applications (with eventual but not too rigorously exploited spinoffs from breakthroughs in military technology). Japan since the early Meiji period (1868–1912) has overwhelmingly stressed applied science in its catch-up role as a technological latecomer. With the U.S. providing the defense umbrella during the Cold War, Japan was able to focus single-mindedly on commercially oriented R & D, thereby widening the gap.

From the mid-1980s both nations started to question their traditional emphases. The U.S. at last woke up to the strategic significance of economic competitiveness and the commercial technology required to underpin it. Japan, unwilling to depend on others in the sharpening competition, realized that economic survival demanded the drastic upgrading of its own infrastructure for basic research. As the two nations begin their technological dos-à-dos, however, there is a structural difference in science and technology research that works greatly to Japan's advantage.

The best scientific work in the United States, especially the basic research now of primary concern to the Japanese, is typically carried out at American universities. These are wide open to foreign participation and unfettered in the dissemination of their research product, which is normally in the public domain as professors rush their latest discoveries into print. In Japan it is the other way around. The best-equipped research facilities and the frontline work in commercial R & D (now of belated interest to Americans) are to be found in the corporate laboratories, where information is largely proprietary (as in private sectors everywhere) and, in Japan, very closely guarded. In short, while Japanese researchers have the free run of those U.S. institutions of greatest benefit to their country's national objectives, Americans find that the Japanese facilities of greatest significance for their own national interest are the very ones most closed to outsiders.

For decades Japan's better-equipped laboratories—those run by private corporations and government agencies—were off limits to foreigners. Until recently the sole experience open to American researchers in Japan has been in the poorly appointed, shamefully dilapidated university laboratories, most of them not refurbished for the last twenty or thirty years. Many foreign visitors have been even more critical of the noncreative research ambience in these academic facilities with their group focus, their rigid hierarchical ties between senior professors and younger staff, the stifling administrative chores foisted on junior researchers, and their clannish avoidance of horizontal ties to business or government, or to scholars at other universities.

Intersectoral cooperation in Japan has improved over the past decade, and from the late 1980s government and private labs gingerly began to open their doors to foreigners. As in the U.S., work that must be carried out on a national scale has been entrusted to government-funded special corporations (e.g., in space development or nuclear energy) or to laboratories attached to governmental ministries and agencies (e.g., in agriculture or transportation). Most of Japan's cutting-edge commercial R & D, however, remains tightly held within vertically integrated corporate structures, in horizontally linked *keiretsu* cartels that minimize wasteful overlap, and by companies that participate in privately based "technological research associations."[9] Foreign analysts have been especially critical of the lack of openness and transparency in industry-wide research projects promoted by MITI for the development of precommercial technologies of seminal significance in areas such as optoelectronics and sixth-generation computers.[10]

Proprietary attitudes toward information extend to many types of government and academic data that in the U.S. normally would be in the public domain—such as nonclassified military information or routine social survey statistics collected by government institutes.[11] The concept of the public's right to know (*shiru kenri*) is very new to Japan, where the underlying assumption has been that information (which conveys power) is privileged unless there are convincing reasons why it should not be. Bureaucrats hoard information at the ministerial or even departmental level, and some of the difficulty of foreign access derives from this pervasive sectionalism. There is also the sheer inertia of a society that has not stressed horizontal information flows—where the so-called "gray literature" of nonrestricted but poorly distributed publications piles up in the offices of government agencies, private think tanks, and academic conference organizers. Bi-governmental efforts to improve U.S. access to Japanese data have been directed mainly at this inertial level. The Japan Documentation Center of the Library of Congress was established in 1994 with the support of the Japan Foundation's Center for Global Partnership, and the machine translation center for Japanese scientific documents was set up in Washington in 1995 with joint funding from Japan's Science and Technology Agency.

The ultimate key to righting the balance, however, lies in giving American scientists and engineers working in Japan the same opportunity for long-term stays and permanent positions that have enabled Japanese researchers to participate fully in America's science and technology mainstream. That means opening the way for what one might call the "reverse Tonegawas" of the future—an American who someday might win the Nobel Prize from a tenured post in Japan, something totally unthinkable today. One still hears Tokyo's counter-complaint that not many Americans want to come, but this needs to be placed in its historical context. The *relative* lack of interest on the American side should not be allowed to exonerate administrative or attitudinal barriers on the part of the Japanese toward those who do want to participate.

For decades Western humanists and social scientists have found Japan an intellectually relevant, if professionally frustrating, place. A fair number of them have stayed on either as specialists in their own languages and cultures, for which they find an extensive market, or as scholars of Japan or nearby Asia, in which case the land itself serves as their principal "laboratory" and "database." Until very recently, however, Japan has not been a popular destination with American natural scientists and engineers, who, like scientists anywhere, tend to be motivated by strictly qualitative criteria when choosing to work in a foreign country. For decades the United States has offered the most advanced frontiers of research, the finest physical facilities, and the most hospitable and unrestricted professional ambience in the world. In addition to the language problem, the logistics of transplanting one's family, and the fear of staying outside the Stateside "loop" too long—disincentives that persist today—there was for too long a belief that there was not much to be learned in or from Japan.

Research in basic science throughout the world normally is conducted by scholar-teachers and full-time researchers on the permanent staffs of major universities. Unfortunately for those foreign scientists willing and able to work in Japan for the long term, the same limitations on permanent appointments that we have analyzed in Chapter 3 apply to scientific researchers at Japan's national universities (the private campuses hardly count) and at laboratories under the jurisdiction of the Monbusho. There has been little meaningful progress on those barriers since 1985 when Tokyo mandated its fresh emphasis on basic research and enhanced international interchange to sustain it. In 1988 three American scholars at the National Laboratory for High Energy Physics (KEK) at Tsukuba wound up their interview with the *Japan Times* as follows:

[Interviewer] So is there any hope for researchers seeking long-term positions?

[American #1] People who have tried to get permanent positions here have been pretty poorly treated. I've been treated like a prince.

[American #2] You're just visiting, that's different. But for people who want to come here and take permanent positions, it's hopeless. . . . Foreigners who come here with the intention of doing research for a longer period of time would require some sort of job security, but that's impossible. Well, I know why: They reserve the permanent positions for their own cronies—absolutely! That's the way the system works.[12]

The handbook for visiting U.K. researchers issued by the British Chamber of Commerce in Japan (BCCJ) in 1990 carried one former exchangee's warning to the effect that, "There are virtually no opportunities for full-time employment in Japanese academia on completion of a fellowship there." The stark alternatives suggested were: go home or elsewhere; find work in Japan's private sector; derail into something like Tokyo-based science journalism; or keep trying to come back on short-term fellowships.[13] That is not what the most promising Japanese researchers have to put up with in the United States. Surveys of foreign scientists in Japan for the short term reveal the standard mix of positive notes on things like initial Japanese hospitality and a sense of adventure and challenge, together with a growing sense of personal and professional isolation as time moves on and, in many instances, the awareness of having been kept on the periphery of the main action.[14]

Given this lack of long-term prospects, and the barriers to a more natural and undirected inflow of foreign talent such as takes place in the United States, it is not surprising that most of the American scientific researchers in Japan are there on specially organized, short-term, programs—once again, the "exchange" approach. It is easier both for Tokyo's science and technology establishment and for foreign embassy representatives to negotiate a set of specific opportunities for access than to dismantle the cartelized structure of Japanese research itself. The main pressure for change has come from foreign governments, and short-term exchanges are the typical intergovernmental response. As one veteran British correspondent remarked of MITI's sparkling new Techno-Growth House hostel for visiting researchers in the paddy fields at Tsukuba, "It's the dream come true for every science attaché under pressure from his embassy to show that something is being done. But it does nothing for the actual imbalance. The Japanese told me it was built to please the Americans." Although perhaps too acerbic, that remark captured the

Japanese penchant for bricks and mortar rather than people as the key to *kokusaika*.

As of 1996 officials in both Tokyo and Washington were complaining that American researchers were not making full use of the exchange opportunities now open to them. One U.S. official confided to me, however, that some of Japan's "special" programs were not well structured to appeal to American scientists. Perhaps the problem lies in being *too* structured—procrustean, that is—with respect to the visitors' real research interests. Again, unlike humanists and social scientists for whom the "Japan experience" itself provides a certain stimulative return, the foreign researcher in science and technology can quickly waste a precious year if unable to perform and develop what is often a highly specialized project. Where most Japanese researchers get into American science through the open barn door, Americans in Japan may not feel all that comfortable in their briefly appointed dovecotes and chicken coops.

Scientific exchanges arranged with the help of the U.S. government date back 35 years to the United States–Japan Scientific Cooperation Agreement of 1961. The Cooperative Science Program was designed to facilitate a two-way flow of individuals—mainly to the U.S.—for brief periods of research and seminars in project fields defined by the two administering agencies, the National Science Foundation (NSF) and the Japan Society for the Promotion of Science (JSPS), an adjunct of the Ministry of Education. The tie-ups were exclusively between individual scholars. In 1988, reflecting both advances in science and America's new worries about economic competitiveness, the Agreement was upgraded to an "Umbrella" covering all scientific fields, mandating institution-to-institution ties between the two countries' national research institutes, and encouraging private sector cooperation.[15]

To give some idea of program levels, NSF figures for 1994 showed 809 American researchers, primarily in the areas of science and technology, visiting for one week to a year or more for research or study at Japanese university and government institute facilities. Of these, 422 stayed for up to three months and 201, for a year or more. Undergraduates accounted for 116; those with a master's degree or in graduate programs, for

310; post-docs, nearly all staying over one year, for 121; and senior researchers visiting on cooperative projects (half of them staying up to one month), for 262. The largest contingent (approximately 300) was sent by the 12 U.S.-Japan Industry and Technology Management Training Centers supported at American universities by the Air Force Office of Scientific Research (AFOSR)—a project whose funding was reduced by roughly half in 1995 and which suffered a similar cut in 1996.

The NSF coordinated programs that support 252 fellows, mostly at the doctoral student, Ph.D., and senior researcher levels. Among these noncorporate exchanges there were 141 Americans, mostly senior level, in programs administered directly by the Japanese. Meanwhile, Japan's institutional base for science exchanges had expanded beyond the JSPS to include the Science and Technology Agency, the Research Development Corporation of Japan, the Agency of Industrial Science and Technology under MITI, and others.[16]

Among the programs spawned by the "Umbrella" there are three—including the AFOSR and the Manufacturing Technology Fellowships jointly sponsored by MITI and the Department of Commerce—that have sought to place their grantees in corporate laboratories, and as of 1995 a total of 128 Japanese companies were willing to be listed as potential hosts.[17] Although an earlier survey of such firms in 1991 revealed a general preference for two- to three-year stays, a small minority did express its desire for long-term hires on a renewable-contract basis.[18] Bringing one highly-trained American into a laboratory as a regular employee is less expensive and offers a greater multiplier effect than sending several Japanese staffers abroad. Taking foreign researchers into a company also offers a hedge against the continuing decline in numbers of college-age Japanese, including the annual supply of new scientists and engineers.

In certain niches of Japanese business at least, the idea may be getting through that cross-border pollination in science and technology can be a two-way street. However, as the British advised their own incoming scientists, the extremely rare foreign researcher promoted to a permanent position is most likely to find himself assigned to company-affiliated labs overseas, or to international liaison duties at the home office.[19]

That is to say, he is utilized at least in part for his "foreignness" rather than for his substantive science.

One could hope that the laboratories of private industry—with some sense of the corporate advantage to be had from long-term commitments—might lead a gradual opening of Japan's cartelized research world as American and other Western researchers increase their interest in, and language capability for, extended work in Japan. The key question is whether or not they will be allowed into the upper management and made privy to the most advanced technologies. One litmus test would be the experience of the Asian researchers who have preceded them, and here the preliminary prognosis is not so good. Japan is well known for its strategic reluctance to permit the transfer of cutting-edge technologies to Asian researchers and engineers employed in local Japanese affiliates throughout the region.[20]

Unfortunately, as with all the other intellectual barriers, there are indications that these Japanese patterns may be adopted by neighboring countries. Although the level of Japan's R & D still vastly outpaces the rest of Asia, several factors suggest that imbalances in scientific and technological access and information flows may become a region-wide problem for U.S. policymakers. These factors include sustained regional economic growth, strong government support in many countries for the emerging R & D infrastructure, and a rapidly expanding pool of highly trained researchers. Meanwhile, the U.S. is affording these countries the same opportunities that the Japanese have enjoyed for investing in American start-up companies and evincing the same openness of American universities to Asian students, researchers, tenured professors, and optimally targeted funding. Add to this the growing availability of doctoral-level training, especially in Japan and India, and the antipicated return of increasing numbers of the most talented Asian scientists and engineers to their own country after their training in America.[21]

Clearly the U.S. needs to preempt any spread of Japanese-style research cartelism by establishing a convincing precedent and norm for bilateral reciprocity with the Asian pace-setter, Japan. For this reason, at the meetings of the APEC leaders in

Seattle in 1993 and again in Indonesia in 1994, the American side was quite wary of Tokyo's enthusiasm for moving the question of Japan-U.S. technological cooperation to a multinational level focusing on environmental, energy, and other challenges throughout Asia. It saw this as an attempt by the Japanese to divert attention from bilateral access issues in scientific research and from trade liberalization in general.

FOREIGN STUDENTS: 100,000 SWEET OR SOUR ON JAPAN?

Foreign teachers and researchers are not the only ones kept at arm's length on Japanese university campuses. There is also the younger generation of outsiders—the foreign students, known as *ryugakusei*, both graduate and undergraduate. Attitudinal roots show up most clearly and poignantly here, inasmuch as both parties, Japanese and foreign alike, are still at a relatively open and ingenuous stage of their personal development.

The intellectual "cartelization" of students differs from the others in two major respects. First, in terms of numbers it is fellow Asians rather than Westerners who bear the brunt of Japan's exclusionism. Second, despite major institutional problems, the overriding barrier in this case is attitudinal—a cartel not so much *of* as *in* the mind. The human experience here not only has a profound and lasting impact on young adults, many of whom are destined for the political, business, or academic leadership of their own countries, but it vividly illuminates the insular psychology that informs the more institutionalized cartels in other areas of intellectual activity.

There are three main groups of foreign students who enroll at Japanese universities for purposes of substantive study (as distinct from those who have entered Japan for the sole purpose of learning the Japanese language). Motives for study, levels of cultural preparedness, and the degree of interest in Japan *per se* vary greatly among these three. The largest contingent by far, 41,850 or 77.8 percent of the 53,847 total as of May 1995, are the intensely studious Northeast Asians from China, Taiwan, and South Korea, the majority of them in the social, natural, and applied sciences.[22] As members of the broader Sinitic cultural orbit, they share with their Japanese hosts the use of Chinese characters and the same Confucian-inspired drive toward educational excellence. The best of them are a chosen national elite on full scholarship from their own government (or from Japan's), with assured positions of influence once they return home. As such, they represent a natural revival of the *ryugakusei* pattern of the early twentieth century, when Japan, having developed a modern university system, offered to the nearby Chinese and to its own colonial subjects in Taiwan and Korea a cheaper and linguistically quicker access to the applied sciences and technology than could be had in the West. Except for the occasional Japanologist, these Northeast Asians have about as much interest in a "cultural encounter" with Japan as a Chinese physicist at MIT would have in exploring the Puritan heritage of old Boston.

Similarly enrolled for the full undergraduate course or for a graduate degree are the Southeast Asian *ryugakusei* (about nine percent of the total in 1995), together with a sprinkling of others from former colonial dependencies of the West in South Asia, Africa, and the Near East. Starting (like any American) with no knowledge of Chinese characters, this group of foreign students has proved that it is possible to overcome this reading handicap to complete a Japanese degree course, and they often enjoy a compensating advantage with their previous command of English and their easygoing, self-confident familiarity with Western culture. Culturally "trilateral" by the time they leave Japan, the Southeast Asian *ryugakusei* would be the natural go-betweens in the emerging Asia-Pacific community, were it not for the greater prestige still attaching in their own countries to a higher education in the West, or the reluctance of Japanese firms to remove their "glass ceiling" on executive jobs to permit non-Japanese participation in major corporate decisions.

Ryugakusei from North America and Europe numbered under 2,500 or less than five percent of the total in 1995. The typical undergraduate among them is in Japan precisely for the "Japan experience" rather than for a degree education, while many of the graduate students have come for advanced training as Japanologists. Few Westerners stay longer than for a college year-abroad program or a couple of years of Ph.D. dissertation research, but since the focus of their study is Japan itself, it behooves the Japanese to take seriously these future windows of the Occident onto their own country.

Difficulties facing foreign students in Japan, as in any other country, sort themselves into two basic clusters, the logistical and the personal. On the material side, there are the high cost of living, the lack of scholarship funds and dormitory facilities, the refusal of many landlords to rent to students (particularly from the developing countries), and the difficulty of finding part-time work (acceptable to the immigration authorities) to support an extended period of study. On the human side, one finds the language barrier, the difficulty of making social contact even when fluent, the lack of student counseling services, and the pervasive feeling among non-Caucasians that they are being looked down upon.

Aggravating both the logistical and personal difficulties of *ryugakusei* is Japan's lack of a residential college tradition that would, if it existed, ease the housing, social, and language-learning barriers with one stroke. Because of crowded urban conditions, budgetary restraints, and the strongly utilitarian (as opposed to humanistic) spirit of Japanese higher education ever since the Meiji period, dormitory living has never become an established preference among Japanese students. The minuscule number who from financial necessity do live in the occasional dormitory are likely to find them rather cold and barracks-like places, watched over by superannuated and eagle-eyed wardens. Adding to the impersonality of Japanese campuses that empty out by dinnertime is the tightly knit, intensive, and exclusive character of those student activities where Japanese undergraduate socializing does take place. These include the do-or-die varsity athletic teams (and their equally grim cheerleading squads); the familistic upper-class "seminars" (*zemi*) gathered around their paternalistic professor for two years of joint research, drinking parties, and study outings; and the mutual-interest "circles" ranging from lawn tennis to Shakespeare clubs.

Whereas the process of socialization for American undergraduates is typically a centrifugal, outward-looking dynamic, in Japan it turns the youngster inward toward a narrowly focused and strictly hierarchical group loyalty. This horizontal bonding among classmates is expected to last for a lifetime, and strong vertical ties improve the chances that the older members may someday help to recruit their juniors into their own firms. Foreign students simply do not fit into this matrix. They are mere passing presences who have come, without exception, from countries where the process of "joining" is less demanding, and they rarely have the time, energy, or interest for the total commitment required by Japanese group membership. By the same token, young Japanese have had very little experience of the more spontaneous, individual-to-individual, non-group-referenced friendships sought by the *ryugakusei* of all stripes.

On the material side, to give credit where due, this is the one intellectual arena where Japan has made significant numerical strides toward "opening up." In 1995 Japan was host to nearly 54,000 *ryugakusei*, up from a mere 10,482 in 1983 and more than halfway toward the goal of a foreign student population of 100,000 by the year 2000 that was set by Prime Minister Nakasone in 1985. The logistical problems, too, have been openly acknowledged. Progress has been made in providing greater scholarship assistance from the central government, local authorities, and corporate business; in establishing professionally staffed foreign student advisory services at the universities; and in constructing a certain number of hostels exclusively for the *ryugakusei*.

Unfortunately, special quarters, however attractive, drive yet another wedge between foreign students and Japanese society as a whole. If the Japanese stop with progress on statistically quantifiable problems like finances and accommodations without tackling the psychological roots of foreign student alienation, they run the risk of raising up a Japan-trained subelite in neighboring Asia that will be cool, if not downright resentful, toward their country—much like their own fervidly anti-American, pro-Nazi prewar Foreign Minister, Yosuke Matsuoka, who never forgot the racial slights he had endured in Oregon as a Japanese *ryugakusei*. Indeed, a poll of 488 Asian students in 1988 showed that they felt discriminated against and financially strained, and that only half of them had a favorable view of their decision to study in Japan. Seventy percent of them said it was difficult to make Japanese friends, with a full third reporting no Japanese friends at all.[23] The human and foreign-policy implications of these statistics are ominous. In 1996 a two-page special in the *Asian Wall Street Journal* revealed how many young Mainland, Taiwan, and Hong-Kong Chinese—who had arrived in Japan full of admiration for its economy, enthusiastic for its popular culture, and willing to forget the past—were "completely turned off" by the pervasive discrimination and petty harrassment, and *as a result* of such treatment came to harbor fears of a revival of Japanese militarism.[24]

It is a pity that Japan's educational bureaucrats and the establishmentarian scholars and experts whom they draw into their consultative orbit tend toward the sort of cultural nationalism that stresses the intractable differences between Japanese and outsiders. They nip in the bud that very human empathy and generosity of imagination required as the first step toward solving the "subjective" plight of the foreign students.

One of the most outgoing and well-adjusted of the Southeast Asian students I taught during my ten years as a university professor in Japan wrote in English in his class graduation album that there had been times when he had "wanted someone who would come and talk naturally, not just to practice his poor English." After four years that were "not so great, nor darn bad," he wanted before leaving "to thank those friends who have been 'friends,' who received [me] into a natural circle of friends. They will always be remembered, any time, anywhere."

Fluent in Japanese, but with good English from his year as an exchange student at an American high school, this young man was prey to the English-conversation cultists among his classmates. Having approached dozens of Japanese for the same purpose years ago when I was a beginner in their language, I really cannot fault the instinct. But the young Thai had put his finger on the more subtle and poignant form of student segregation—namely, the reluctance (or inability) of most Japanese undergraduates, even after four years of daily contact, to transcend the we-they consciousness barrier and the mental stance of "here I am having a cultural encounter with a foreigner."

That this barrier is not primarily one of language or race was made clear to me by a Chinese graduate student from the People's Republic who accosted me at one of those Special Receptions for Foreigners. These gatherings, at Christmas or graduation time, are organized by the Japanese university authorities, who feel more comfortable throwing all the outlanders together with a few of the "foreigner-handling" Japanese staff, instead of inviting them to their own, more intimate, departmental celebrations. Briefly brushing by each other are teachers and students from all over the world, most of whom have never seen each other before, and most likely will never meet again. "I'm so happy to have met an American!" the young man gushed, in fluent Japanese. "It's so difficult to have a meaningful conversation with the Japanese," he added by way of explanation. "They never really let you know what's on their mind." But here we were, the two of us, one "communist" Chinese and one American capitalist, with minimal competence in each other's language, chattering away with gusto in the native tongue of our Japanese hosts. If nothing else, we were offering proof positive that their language—even at our level of command—was as suitable as any other for communication between persons of different cultural backgrounds.

Another young Chinese, a graduate in Japanese Studies from a leading mainland Chinese university, was downright bitter in telling me (again, in Japanese) how he and his fellow foreign students, Chinese and Southeast Asian and Peruvian alike, had all—and he stressed the word "all"—"had their fill" (*korigori shita*) of the "narrow-mindedness" (*kokoro no semasa*) of the Japanese. Always hiding behind their *tatemae* (one's overt assertion as opposed to one's true intent), he lamented, it was "impossible to have a real discussion or friendship" with them.

What lies behind this stand-offishness of Japanese collegians toward the foreign students in their midst? If the Japanese have so much difficulty opening their society to the Chinese students, how will they ever win the hearts of *ryugakusei* from more distant parts of Asia, let alone the rest of the world? The best clue to that aloofness is to be found, I think, in the resistance encountered by the so-called *kikokushijo* or "repatriated children" of Japanese parents working abroad, who enter Japanese universities directly from foreign secondary schools. If the foreign *ryugakusei* are like comets, sweeping briefly in and out of Japan's orbit, the *kikokushijo* are more like meteors sending out a final flash of internationalist exuberance before sputtering out in Japan's conformist atmosphere.

Some Western observers have rhapsodized about the catalytic force for internationalization, liberalization, and social change in Japan that these young returnees represent.[25] But after a decade of teaching them and watching their often painful passage to re-Japanization—and to good jobs only after employers are convinced that they will *not* rock the boat—it is an optimism that I do not share. Indeed, a fair number of them wind up working for foreign companies or living a good part of their adult lives abroad.

The *kikokushijo* I had the privilege of teaching were an extraordinary, and extraordinarily charming, lot taken as a whole. There were proper English gentlemen, London-tailored down to their brass-buttoned blue blazers, gray flannel trousers, and clipped West End accents; insouciant howdy-pardners from Texas; scrappy pugilists from high schools in Queens who had been sucked into ethnic gang rumbles on the side of the immigrant Chinese; gracious, socially poised mademoiselles who expressed themselves best in conservatory French or—if one could field it, which I couldn't—the twang of Brazilian Portuguese.

Understandably, there were peer pressures to become more recognizably Japanese. Doing so, however, was not primarily a matter of externals, nor even of language, although there is at least one campus in Tokyo that takes returnees whose Japanese is beyond repair for a college education and places them with foreign students in an all-English-language curriculum. Those I taught were not linguistically handicapped and were working very hard on their rough edges. The real crunch came over their manner of self-expression—indeed, over the legitimacy of self-expression itself. What the returnees found most difficult to suppress, since it had become second nature to them—and what offended their Japanese classmates most—was their carefree and unadulterated proclamation of their own ideas, tastes, and personalities. This was precisely what the stay-at-homes have had drummed out of them in the course of a typical Japanese secondary education. The unbridled individualism of the *kikokushijo* grated on their group-oriented sensitivities, challenging, taunting, perhaps even threatening, the selves that they had labored so hard to bury.

It was more the form than the content of *kikokushijo* expression that bothered them. The Japan-educated student is as capable as any other of outrageous posturings or intellectual heterodoxy—but he or she is always careful to signal the others that, "I'm still with you, this is not *really* me." The cardinal transgression of the returnees was to have declared the independence of their own egos from the group or from whomever they might be talking to. They seemed to have turned themselves inside out for all to see, to have failed to cover their raw intent, or *honne*, with sufficient fig leaves of softening, oblique, face-saving *tatemae*. They had become, in fact, disturbingly like all those pointy-faced, big-nosed, flappy-tongued, intrusive, extrusive, obtrusive Caucasians—or self-expressive Asians—who could never learn to feel what it was really like to be Japanese. Down with "trusiveness"!

In the mid-1990s the U.S. government launched a campaign to increase the flow of American students to Japan—a modest sideshow in the overall *ryugakusei* scene. The new U.S. ambassador, Walter Mondale, had hardly arrived at his post in late 1993 when he called the deficit in student exchanges "the worst imbalance of all"—Japan having 42,840 students in the United States that year as compared to 1,192 Americans studying in Japan, a ratio favoring Japan 36 to one.[26] Apart from the personal loss to American youngsters, to say nothing of Japan's own self-inflicted PR deficit, U.S. officials see the national interest—specifically, the ability to compete—significantly disadvantaged by this one-way flow of knowledge. Whereas young Japanese elites dispatched by their government or corporation can mingle freely with Americans at the most prestigious U.S. universities and colleges, the reverse opportunity is closed to future American leaders who are studying state-of-the-art technologies or who want to learn what makes their country's chief Asian partner and economic rival tick.

In November 1995 both governments finalized a plan to bring 100 (!) American students to Japan for six weeks during the summer of 1996 to attend Japanese language and culture courses in Tokyo and then stay with Japanese families. The Ministry of Education (Monbusho) promised to contribute 34 million yen (about $340,000 at the then exchange rate), Northwest Airlines pledged $1.5 million in airfares, and Senators Richard Lugar and Jay Rockefeller exhorted U.S. officials and corporate executives to support a greater flow of American students to Japan. The Association of American Colleges and Universities joined with other educational groups in a longer-term "Bridging Project" to recruit students and study ways of overcoming the main obstacles, which were defined by those involved in the project as an insufficiency of money, information, and knowledgeable faculty mentors. A database accessible to students through the Internet would be created, and work was to continue on problems of visa facilitation, housing, transfers of credit, and the development of English-language curricula on Japan both in the U.S. and at Japanese national universities willing to set up special courses for visiting Americans.[27]

Brought into being by the persistent entreaties of the American side of the bi-governmental advisory Conference on Cultural and Educational Interchange (CULCON), this new project starts out as little more than an enhanced summer-study program—of which there are already several sponsored by U.S. and Japanese universities alike. Admittedly, the enormous lag in language training on the U.S. side, and the fact that few Americans are motivated to stay in Japan for a full degree course (be it the B.A., M.A., or Ph.D.), make it a foregone conclusion that the numbers will never reach anywhere near parity. As with the American researchers, however, that does not absolve the Japanese from removing obstacles on their side. Given the less flexible organization of Japanese universities for receiving foreign students, and the persistence of certain legal "structural" barriers, it is much easier for a Japanese student, even with barely acceptable English, to move in and out of regular American college or graduate programs (to say nothing of the many short-term intensive language schools) for a year or two than it is for a linguistically prepared and highly motivated American to attempt anything similar in Japan.

In 1994 the Oiso Kenkyukai, a blue-ribbon binational study group of twelve professionals representing the key governmental and private organizations in Japan-U.S. graduate, collegiate, and high-school exchanges, recommended "deregulation" in four problem areas. They called for granting legal status under Japanese civil law to foreign nongovernmental organizations (NGOs) conducting exchanges in Japan; the enactment of new legislation to permit tax-free contributions by Japanese business and create a more favorable tax status for foreign NGOs; the introduction of additional and more flexibly applied visa categories to accommodate a greater diversity of foreign student programs; and the repeal (or replacement with certified bank balances) of the complicated guarantor requirements now burdening the individual Japanese sponsor, usually a university staff member or the host family head.[28]

The most natural "balance," the most genuine "reciprocity," would emerge if Japanese officials would simply lower all these artificial barriers and allow American students to sink or swim on the strength of their own commitment—and that of their American backers—as Japanese students do in the United States. Unfortunately, at any call for hard-core regulatory changes the cartel mentality freezes. Not surprisingly, these four proposals have met with little enthusiasm on the Japanese side of CULCON, which feels more comfortable with a less demanding soft-core agenda covering language, scholarships, housing, and curriculum. As one former Monbusho official put it with refreshing candor: "Naturally until very recent times, Japanese universities have not been expected to provide education for students from 'advanced countries' who are not potential workers within the framework of Japanese society. . . . The Japanese education system has long been designed for the purpose of training manpower for the Japanese society alone."[29] The nationalistic, utilitarian voice of that system's Meiji-period founders remains vibrant and unreconstructed a century later.

A more visible activity from the late 1980s onward has been the effort to establish branch university and college campuses in each other's country—another experiment endorsed by CULCON in the name of "regionalizing" exchanges at the "grass roots" level. Promoting the American branches in Japan were Japanese politicians who touted them as a wedge for "internationalization"; U.S. officials who thought that the sale of "educational services" could somehow help the trade balance; American university administrators in search of additional students and tuition; local Japanese civic boosters and commercial entrepreneurs with their eye on a quick profit; and Japanese students who had failed to enter the better universities or were drawn by the possibility of transferring later to the American home campus. Burgeoning to more than 30 campuses in Japan during the 1990–1991 academic year—many of them small community colleges with no real counterpart in the Japanese higher education system—their numbers plummeted to a mere handful by the mid-1990s. Although two or three of these institutions have found a genuinely functional niche— most notably Temple University's thriving campus in Tokyo, and the remote but locally popular branch of Minnesota State University in Akita prefecture—the great majority of them have closed in a cacaphony of mutual recriminations over defaulting commercial sponsors, low student interest, poor American planning, and Japanese parents demanding their money back.

The Japanese campuses in America—rather like the overseas outposts maintained by many American universities—capitalize on the cachet of an education in the United States (without, organizationally speaking, ever leaving home). In both countries these branches were developed almost exclusively for Japanese collegians, with relatively little participation by American students. Unfortunately, at a time when Japanese corporations were snapping up exclusive golf courses and other U.S. real estate trophies, certain Japanese universities—of uniformly lower quality—managed to buy out venerable but impecunious American liberal arts colleges and turn them into physical extensions of their own cramped urban campuses, with minimal educational or social ties to their American setting.[30]

This sadly failed regional push illustrates two other emphases in Japan's "cultural exchange" (*bunka koryu*) approach that serve to deflect a more penetrating or permanent foreign presence in the central and "ordinary" channels of Japanese intellectual life. First, the Japanese tend to stress the short-term gimmick. And, second, they prefer creating special or *extra*ordinary programs rather than providing direct access to Japan's mainline institutions.

Japanese officials and private do-gooders alike repeatedly substitute *bunka koryu* —with its inherent tangentiality and its in-again-out-again, hello-and-goodbye, short-term ratchet—for "internationalizing" or opening the country itself. As I suggested in Chapter 3, the "cultural exchange" approach (which does have legitimate short-term goals) too often camouflages a lack of genuine *kokusaika*, a refusal to dismantle the cartels of the mind for the long run. One need only recall the annual one-week journalists' junket for prominent foreign editors; the university policies terminating foreign instructors after three years in the name of "variety"; and the special dormitories for foreign students and luxury hostels for visiting researchers. One American writer on a fellowship in Tokyo tried to enroll his two sons in the neighborhood Japanese elementary school only to be advised to apply to another district since, "We just had our year for *kokusaika* last year."[31] In their focus on the short term, the Japanese seem to forget that, out of every hundred young foreigners left dazzled by a six-week all-expense-paid trip to their country, two or three may decide to commit themselves for the long run; and that those who embark on a business, legal, academic, or reporter's career related to Japan will eventually— with consternation and resentment—run afoul of one or another of the cartel-type barriers.

Finally, special facilities and programs to accommodate foreigners or to lend a "foreign" touch, however welcome to those visitors who enjoy them, simply postpone the genuine opening of Japan's leading institutions for teaching and research. Indeed, the most pernicious puffery of all concerns new Japanese schools of very minor significance in remote locations that have been hawked as evidence of *kokusaika*.

At *Nature* magazine's 125th anniversary conference in Tokyo in December 1994, a former president of Tokyo University boasted to an assemblage including some of the world's leading university presidents, rectors, and vice-chancellors—none of whom could have known the context—that at the new university at Aizu in northern Honshu nearly half the staff was foreign. The reference was to a new prefectural-level school consisting of two departments for computer hardware and software, with a total student body of 272—the foreign instructors being there for the indispensable language training and the loading and downloading of English-language programs only. Much the same thing could be said of the egregiously mislabeled International University of Japan—a high-quality but tiny private graduate-level institution tucked away in the snow country of Niigata Prefecture. It has two departments offering an M.A. in international relations or international management and a student body of slightly over 200 drawn mainly from young Japanese corporate officials and *ryugakusei* from the developing countries of Asia.

None of the above is intended to demean the honest work that such institutions do, but merely to indicate the way they have been exploited by Japan's cultural spokesmen to suggest a process of "internationalization," or an emulation effect, that would be significant only if it were taking place at Japan's premier universities. It is as though American academe were to claim it was going global by establishing a new college with a large foreign staff in Zap, N.D.—with my apologies to Zap and North Dakota.

5

MANIPULATED DIALOGUE
Cowing the Critics

Japan's barriers to foreign professionals have psychological as well as structured institutional dimensions, as we have seen in each of the intellectual activities thus far surveyed. One final barrier, this one mainly *in* the mind, lies in the way Japanese intellectuals and cultural spokesmen manipulate their dialogue with the outside world to deflect scrutiny, put down criticism, and raise false hopes of intellectual decartelization.

All nations, of course, are inclined to promote favorable images of themselves. This is an occupational disease hardly limited to Tokyo's cultural and foreign-policy officials. Where the Japanese differ from the other industrial democracies is not in the way they trumpet their national achievements, but in their strenuous efforts to hide the darker side. Their official spokesmen and unofficial international interlocutors are also determined to contain and guide the external dialogue with other peoples—normally the enterprise of thousands of unstructured and free-thinking individuals—within a range of topics, images, ideas, conclusions, and participants that furthers the Japanese national interest as they have defined it.

This is the opposite of the philosophical approach most clearly expressed in the history of Britain's informational and cultural diplomacy. The BBC enjoyed a unique credibility during World War II thanks to its impartial reporting of battle-field setbacks as well victories, and during the Falkland War of 1982—overriding Tory objections—even went so far as to give equal time to spokesmen for the Argentine government. The British Council, the U.K.'s cultural arm, takes pride in its full portrayal of British life, "warts and all," in the belief that the unvarnished truth is the best guarantor of trust, which in turn is the prerequisite for good will. This is the conceptual corner that the Japanese have been unwilling turn: to see the causal connection between honesty, credibility, and friendship—in that order. The old canards that the fudged truth is safer, that what you don't know can't hurt you, and that intellectual rigging can somehow create genuine good will, are alive and well in Tokyo.

Japan's intellectual defenses draw less on modern propaganda techniques than on approaches the Japanese have long used to manage the truth among themselves.

One of these is the socially lubricating notion that if something embarrassing is not known, or if there is a consensus not to talk about it, then, for all practical purposes, it does not exist. The eye picks it up, of course, but the mind declines to register it on one's consciousness of the overall scene—as audiences at the Kabuki theater do with those assistants (known as *kuroko*) in black hoods and tunics who scurry around the stage changing or adjusting the actors' costumes, seen yet unseen. That is why the foreign observer who openly points to blemishes the Japanese have decided not to discuss is greeted with shock and resentment and quickly becomes a candidate for the *mura hachibu*, or ostracism, that they impose on fellow Japanese who dare to challenge the taboos. At a tea ceremony, after all, one does not probe into a neighbor's daughter's recent abortion.

Japan's official spokesmen and ordinary citizens also have a penchant for personalizing and emotionalizing the ties between nations on the pattern of their own interpersonal relations. This helps to explain why Tokyo's negotiators so often resort to "national sentiment" (*kokumin kanjo*) as an implicit threat at the bargaining table; why so much beguiling personal kindness, flattery, and VIP treatment is lavished on prominent individuals from (or in) other countries in hopes of buying their restraint, or even changing their views, instead of genuinely addressing their grievances; why so much public-relations treacle gets spread around in the name of "friendship" and "mutual understanding"; and why the fun suddenly stops and gives way to intimidation or sullen stonewalling when the game no longer seems to be working.

Undergirding all the taboos and personalization is the sense in Japan—honed to a finer point than elsewhere—of information as a political resource to be guarded, exploited, and distributed in general accordance with the national interest by those charged with the tending of that interest. We are speaking here less about hard scientific knowledge and technological secrets than about the social, economic, and political information—including facts, perceptions, and ideas—that constitute the public discourse in a modern nation. To be fair, Japan's postwar constitution, court rulings, and the increasing demand of the media, voting public, and foreign governments for greater bureaucratic "transparency" are all slowly pushing in the right direction, despite the absence of American-style "sunshine" legislation. What does remain in place as a distant legacy of the perfected information management of the Tokugawa shogunate (as I would argue) is the continuing docility and willing capacity for self-censorship that comes into play with major issues affecting the national interest (such as the trade surplus) or national sensitivities (like the responsibility of the late Emperor Hirohito for the Pacific War). Huddled together in silence among themselves, the Japanese will close ranks even more tightly when the questioning, scrutiny, and criticism are levelled from the outside.

It has been a staple of writing on Japan for the past hundred years that the Japanese make a more conscious and accepted distinction between official truths and actuality than do most other peoples, although they hardly have a patent on it. The political magnitude of Japan's better known dual-track realities, however, can be quite breathtaking. A national textbook screening system has for half a century cosmeticized Japan's role in World War II. Social discrimination against a long since legally nonexistent outcaste group, the so-called *burakumin*, persists.

Many taboos still deter too close a scrutiny or discussion of the Imperial family. Awkward public silences and denials for several years delayed a concerted attack on the AIDS threat.

CULTURAL EXCHANGE AS CULTURAL BUFFERING

Regrettably, the inclination to block serious participation by foreigners in Japan's cartels of the mind—a reflex we have traced all the way from high-priced lawyers to impecunious undergraduates—also pervades the one activity we reasonably might hope would be free of it: the cultural exchange business itself.

As an enterprise, of course, the quantity and variety of Tokyo's official cultural diplomacy have expanded exponentially since the early 1970s, with a dramatic rise in corporate involvement from the late 1980s. Although the number of overseas cultural centers remains minuscule, scholarships for the study of Japanese language and culture and funding for artistic presentations abroad have reached very respectable levels. Much of this was in response to prodding by Western governments and exchange organizations no longer willing to carry so much of the bilateral flow with an affluent Japan on their own account.

What concerns us here, rather, are the quality, reciprocity, and interpersonal chemistry of the dialogue supported by this growing commitment to cultural relations. Japan's restraints on an open flow of ideas and on genuinely unfettered exchanges are as much a matter of intellectual *atmospherics*—of polite hints and demurrals, and of simple intentions to obstruct—as of the practical budgetary and logistical *mechanics* of cultural exchange programs. This never-never land of cultural buffering in the name of cultural exchange has to be personally encountered in order to be believed. It was my direct exposure to it as an American university representative and U.S. cultural official in Tokyo that first taught me to look beyond the annual statistics and glossy brochures.

During my consultancy for the Harvard-Yenching Institute from 1971 to 1975, and especially over my eight years as the first Japan representative of the Japan-U.S. Friendship Commission from 1977 to 1984, I became increasingly skeptical of the willingness or ability of many Japanese cultural institutions to participate wholeheartedly in international exchange. Individual scholars and artists, and the occasional drama company or museum, threw themselves at the task with extraordinary enthusiasm. More often than not, however, Japan's cultural panjandrums and appointed monitors of binational exchange seemed more effective in blocking than in facilitating projects that threatened to cut too deeply into established ways, or to lift the drapes too openly.

It may sound incredible that Japan, which complains so loudly about being wrongly or insufficiently understood by others, should want to draw the veil even in the gentler, nonpolitical, realms of the spirit—in the arts, in scholarship, and in the encounter of ideas. The reason, of course, is that there is a great deal here, too, that the Japanese feel has to be protected—and if it is to be "understood" by others, then only with the proper interpretation, that is to say, on Japan's own terms.

The notion of a qualified or manipulated flow of ideas of course undermines the very essence of cultural and intellectual interchange as conceived of by the rest of the advanced industrialized democracies. Even in the often bumpy U.S.-Soviet exchanges and dialogues—like the famous Nixon-Khrushchev "kitchen debate" of 1959—both sides were inclined to square off openly, without pretending to be something other than what they really were. The Japanese term *rikai*, regularly translated in English as "understanding," actually conveys only the sense of an affirmative understanding—that is to say, "acceptance," an indulgence of the other party as it actually is, or as it would like to be seen. This distinction is seldom perceived by the West's cultural interlocutors with Japan, who, applying the standard of their own countries, assume that the Japanese also mean by "understanding" not a forbearing emotional empathy but a clinical, objective, intellectual grasp of the partner nation in all its lights and shadows.

This cultural cloaking, which shuts off free discussion of certain topics most of the world would consider quite factual if not downright academic, rests on the complacent premise that the rest of the world is so ignorant of Japan, or so incapable of comprehending what it does learn, that no great harm will be done to international trust or to intellectual credibility by shutting off a few inconvenient avenues of inquiry.

The simplest yet most fundamental sort of self-veiling is that of the thoughts, feelings, and personalities of those Japanese individuals who themselves are active in cultural interchange. The most poignant case I recall involved a fellow Asian trained in Japan, through the Japanese language, in Japanese Studies, and by Japanese scholars—that is to say, one of their own.

"They came here as a group," the young Thai scholar lamented. "They spent hours debriefing me and my colleagues on our experiences since we left Japan. We told them everything they wanted to know. But they never opened up their own hearts or minds to us. They never told us what they themselves were thinking. It made me feel very sad."

This conversation took place in the mid-1970s at a university in Bangkok that I visited on behalf of the Harvard-Yenching Institute. The young Thai scholar had spent four years in Japan, winning a master's degree and returning to his country as one of its most promising and enthusiastic new specialists in Japanese Studies. When I saw him he had just been grilled by a team of Japanese scholars dispatched by their government to survey the experiences and prospects of former *ryugakusei* from Southeast Asia after returning home. He felt that he had been put under the microscope without being humanly engaged by the junketing group—despite his lengthy Tokyo sojourn. Since I personally knew and admired most of the Japanese group, I was saddened by his story, too, which encapsulates an all-too-common failing among Japan's managers of cultural exchange.

In a second encounter my Japanese intellectual friends were willing to be open—one step forward; but only on the condition that other Japanese would not find out about it—one step back. The occasion, in the early 1970s, was one in which an informal cross-disciplinary medical and social-science research group at Tokyo University, with encouragement from scholars at Harvard, had set out to explore possible applications of modern psychiatry to Japanese history. Invited to the Tokyo sessions as their Harvard liaison, I was treated to an exhilarating intellectual ride as a number of prominent Japanese of the past two hundred years were placed, so to speak, on the couch: epileptoid prime ministers (so the diagnosis went); schizoid literati; emperors, even (gingerly); and some of the putatively depressive personalities like the Tokugawa "peasant sage" Sontoku Ninomiya (the great prewar role model of diligence and frugality) who had helped to saddle modern Japan with its yo-heave-ho work ethic. The psychiatrists in the group were amateur historians and the historians amateur psychologists, and the whole thing eventually foundered on some methodological quibbles from the Harvard Medical School.

I was taken aback, however, when the Tokyo University organizer admonished us that no Japanese outside our circle of half a dozen should even know of the undertaking. It was still too sensitive an issue to probe that deeply, in public, into the national psyche. As one of our most fertile-minded younger participants, himself in charge of a major psychiatric ward, blurted out to me in a private moment, "I don't want to precipitate the collapse of Japan!" This left me dumbfounded. It was as if someone had suggested that Erik Erikson's seminal psychohistorical study of Martin Luther somehow might undermine the Protestant confession, or a Freudian analysis of Lincoln's melancholia, bring down the United States.

Japan's consensual taboos on "sensitive" subjects surfaced more officially at a seminar hosted by the International House of Japan in the late 1980s as part of a major government-funded study on Japan's role in the 1990s. Speaking before the initial meeting of their subcommittee on "internationalization," I was stunned once again by the head scholar's surmise that the subject of *wakon* ("Japanese spirit" or "soul of Japan") would be inappropriate for treatment in the prospective study. It was in the name of that "Japanese spirit," and to protest its degradation, that the novelist Yukio Mishima committed suicide in 1971—and for the alleged neglect of which ex-Prime Minister Nakasone (of all people) received a death threat from the ultra-right in 1988. Yet *wakon*—also known as *Yamato damashii*—is precisely what needs to be put on the table openly, for to it cling all those notions of national uniqueness that are claimed to exempt Japan from the more general rules of humanity, and that require keeping the rest of the world at bay. *Wakon*, however, strikes a very deep nerve, something close perhaps to religious faith in Christianity or Islam—absolute, ineffable, and no more fit for clinical dissection than, say, the Virgin Mary or, as Salman Rushdie was to learn, the Koran. The very root of Japanese identity, in other words, precludes that modicum of rational universalism required as the first step in relating to others through intellectual exchange.

As "internationalization" (*kokusaika*) became the buzzword of Japan's cultural-exchange professionals from the early 1980s, too many of them found yet another handle for procrastination in the *chosa*, or "investigative inquiry"—that is to say, in studying the issue to death. In most modern nations the desirability of becoming more open to the world and "international" would hardly seem to require special research and analysis. Japanese planners and opinion-setters, however, too often tie themselves up in consultative knots—much like the proverbial man at the curb who fails to cross a road for agonizing over the first step. Rather than acting on "internationalization"— however awkward or fraught with initial mistakes—they put off the evil day with an interminable stream of inconclusive and redundant committee reports on the subject.

Nor does straightforward input from foreign resource persons avail when the message is unwelcome, as I discovered in my own deposition to a group that had been assembled under the aegis of the Economic Planning Agency to "study" the requirements for "internationalization" in 1987. My forthright, though politely phrased, criticisms of the state of openness to foreign faculty and students at Tsukuba University (where I had just taught for over two years) produced a palpable discomfort among the Japanese panelists, one of whom asked me if I couldn't find something positive to say about the university. Trying to oblige, I managed a pat on the back for the quality of Tsukuba's students and its brand-new physical plant, but since the subject under discussion was *kokusaika*, all that was quite beside the point. The Japanese committee, however, wanted to be left with a sweetener, with a consensual mix of pluses and minuses, with the subjective feeling that things were basically all right. Once again, an unflattering analysis of one particular aspect of one particular Japanese institution was being taken far too personally, and nationalistically, as a criticism of Japan—indeed, of *wakon*—itself.

Resident foreigners who are fluent in Japanese and willing to confirm the Japanese in their self-image of the day—whether it be uniqueness, victimhood, or consensual harmony—or to at least remain bland and uncontroversial, can make a handsome side income from seminar and panel appearances on the *kokusaika* advisory circuit. But little of this advances the ostensible purpose of these investigative groups. Indeed, the foreign expert too often is brought in simply to affix a prestigious seal of approval to a conclusion already agreed upon by the Japanese organizers. More than once I have sensed an influential Japanese group reaching out toward me as a potential in-house, lapdog intellectual. I have found that the safest way to avoid selling out is to say exactly what you think—say it as graciously as possible; but do not be afraid to say it. Alas, this is not easily done in a society that envelops you with flattery, kindness, and a sense of being needed as long as you play the game—but that can quickly shove you to the sidelines if you don't.

These veilings, annoying enough at the individual level, become truly problematical when they involve major exchange programs of the U.S. government funded over the years with millions of American taxpayer dollars. I confine myself to three examples from the media, artistic and academic exchanges that I helped launch for the Japan-U.S. Friendship Commission. My purpose is not to disparage the projects themselves, which had their modest successes, but to question the cartel-manager reflexes of Tokyo's cultural bureaucrats, whose standpattism and intervention kept some of the Commission's new initiatives from reaching their full potential.

From 1978 through 1992 the JUSFC made annual grants in the range of $50,000 to $100,000 to the Tokyo office of the San Francisco-based Asia Foundation to set up and operate a translation service center that would provide Americans with unvarnished opinions from Japan—that is to say, with an opportunity to listen in on what the Japanese were actually saying to each other. For years the Japanese (through their own efforts, to be sure) have been enjoying a broad access to the American intellectual scene through their unflagging and widely published translations of controversial opinions from American newspapers, magazines, and scholarly journals. They were not so eager, however, to have their own intramural debates tapped directly from the outside, preferring to reveal themselves to overseas readers indirectly through specially commissioned articles written either by sympathetic foreign Japanologists, or by Japanese adept at hitting the right notes for a non-Japanese audience. Hearing of our ambition to replicate the direct pipeline Japanese readers have to America's domestic disputation—much of which, as a matter of course, is unflattering to the United States—one of Tokyo's leading cultural interlocutors confided to me, "Well, that might create another type of misunderstanding." With lower reader interest and fewer all-purpose opinion journals on the American side, the translation service fell short of its original goal, but it was discouraging to hear a former administrative vice minister of the Education Ministry— the most powerful position in Japanese education—express anxiety that such a project might lead to the wrong kind of *rikai*.

Artistic exchanges were the most fun. In contrast to the funereal black or navy-blue suits at academic conferences I had attended as the Commission's representative—a sartorial legacy of the Confucian solemnity that attached to the scholar's role in traditional Japan—the *vernissages* at Tokyo's galleries were a riot of peacocks and popinjays in purple turtlenecks and green leather jackets. Fortunately, there was a lively minority of more youthful patrons and private museums that eventually gave a good showing to American painting and sculpture over the past hundred years. But to most of Japan's cultural and museum officials, bilateral exchange meant swapping Japanese traditional art for European masterpieces housed in U.S. collections. They could break their backs to clear Buddhist statues for display in New York or L.A., but heads would droop and eyes glaze over at any suggestion of a Japanese tour of modern American paintings.

Anything requiring the cooperation of the Cultural Affairs Agency (Bunkacho), an arm of the Ministry of Education, quickly tied one up like Laocoön in the serpents of red tape. An agreement we had drafted for a modest exchange with the

Agency, to bring five Americans artists to Japan annually in cooperation with the National Endowment for the Arts, had to be sent for clearance to the Treaty Bureau of the Ministry of Foreign Affairs. Our offer to supplement Bunkacho grants to Japanese artists dispatched to the United States ran afoul of rigidly pre-set itineraries that, for example, confined a Japanese potter for months on end to Manhattan even when he or she later discovered that the most appropriate master and kiln were in Tennessee. At intervals, suave and ostensibly sympathetic Bunkacho bigwigs were trotted out to commiserate with us over the obtuseness of lower Agency officials in charge of budget and planning, and to aver that something would have to be done about it. Like an ordinary trade dispute, however, several years of American pleading and Japanese promises failed to loosen the Agency's bind on travel orders that would allow Japanese grantees a richer, because more flexible, experience of the American art world.

The most egregious instance of bureaucratic undermining of exchanges occurred when the Monbusho cancelled a modest program of Commission-funded lectureships in American Studies. This program had been requested by the leading Japanese scholars in the field, duly negotiated and funded by the Friendship Commission, and successfully implemented over a period of two years by four national universities that otherwise had limited course offerings on the United States.

Teaching of American history, politics, economics, and society at the undergraduate level in Japan still lags behind what is offered in Japanese Studies in the U.S. There has been a dramatic expansion since the 1970s in the number and disciplinary spread of lecture courses specifically on Japan that are now offered by American universities. This has been achieved thanks to the missionary zeal of American Japanologists, the absence of bureaucratic restrictions, and the influx of millions of dollars in Japanese corporate and government donations no one has hesitated to take. Although college-age Japanese have fairly wide access to general information about the United States, through the media and from survey courses like comparative politics, Japan's universities have been slow to establish tenured chairs or disciplinary courses on exclusively American subjects. The sole exception is American literature, with its quaint but persistent surfeit of Melville and Hawthorne. Occasional attempts to strengthen the curriculum (as opposed to scholarly research) on the U.S. have been stymied by personal cliquism, the vested interests of Europeanists, the ideological hangups of Marxist academics, and above all the Monbusho's reluctance to open new positions in its inflexible academic-chair system for national universities.

Responding to the entreaty of Japan's most noted Americanists, the Friendship Commission inaugurated a mini-project of intensive one-week courses (with a semester's credit) on American subjects that took scholars from some of Japan's most prestigious campuses to outlying universities in places like Okinawa, at a bargain-basement cost to the U.S. taxpayer of about $1,000 per course. (Mind you, these were *Japanese* professors, not Americanists from the U.S.) Matters were proceeding to everyone's satisfaction when, without any notice to the Friendship Commission, the Monbusho in 1982 abruptly ordered the four universities to stop taking American money in support of this effort. The Japanese doyen of American Studies who had requested the project in the first place, and another former administrative vice minister of the Monbusho known for his "internationalizing" views, promised to look into the matter, but half a year went by without any movement or even a report on the issue, which was finally resolved without their assistance—thanks to a truly bizarre "misunderstanding."

By sheer chance I came across the Education Ministry's international bureau chief, a diplomat on secondment from the Foreign Ministry, who was at the U.S. embassy one day on totally unrelated business. When I taxed him over this issue and reminded him of all that our Commission, a federal agency, had been doing for Japanese Studies in the United States, he asked me rather anxiously whether I intended to make the issue political. The thought had not even crossed my mind, but in my surprise I uttered an inarticulate grunt that he apparently mistook for a powerful affirmative. Not a week later, the diplomat phoned to say the matter had been resolved. I called on a young deputy section chief at the Monbusho, who—dispensing with the customary cup of green tea and the shabby little couch reserved for most visitors—had me sit on a rickety chair in front of his desk like a supplicant from the provinces. He muttered darkly about not wanting to open the door to Korean money, too, and handed me a briefly scrawled note reinstating the program. Recalling the $75,000 we were spending annually on bringing Japan's prefectural education officials to the U.S. and sending their counterparts in American states to visit Japan, it was all I could do to keep my diplomatic cool. After all, over a million dollars a year in American tax-payers' money, nearly half the Friendship Commission's annual grants budget at that time, was being spent on the promotion of Japanese Studies in the United States.

As individuals, one of the most extraordinary lapses of Japanese intellectuals active in the cultural-exchange business has been their conspiracy of silence over the treatment of foreign university staff as recounted in Chapter 3. At the governmental level, a once-in-a-lifetime opportunity to mount official exchanges with America on a genuinely disinterested and credible basis was squandered in 1991 when the Foreign Ministry insisted on retaining full control of the new $350 million Center for Global Partnership fund for exchanges with the U.S. In doing so, it brushed aside the strong recommendation of the fund's American advisory board that it be set up as an independent U.S. foundation along the lines of the German Marshall Fund, a gift from the West German government to the American people in 1972. Susan Berresford, vice president of the Ford Foundation, warned that "many knowledgeable people in the U.S." were afraid that the fund might "set U.S.-Japan relations back rather than advance them. Some fear the new foundation will be set up and run with the express purpose of polishing the Japanese image rather than being a legitimate philanthropy in the American tradition."[1]

The official Japanese position was conveyed by the Foreign Ministry's cultural chief, Kazuo Ogura, who, while averring that he wanted the fund "to do new things, and to be imaginative, creative, and perhaps even controversial," was quick to add that an overly independent fund might "strike out a certain independent, individualistic, unorthodox or controversial policy" unacceptable to his government. "The fund," he insisted, "will have to strike a balance."[2]

A balance between PR and autonomy, we can only infer—lest the new fund kick over the traces of Japan's restrictive and manipulative cultural-exchange cartel and open up a genuinely unfettered dialogue.

DISCREDITING DISSENT

When you can't parry the message, put down the messenger. That was the essence of Japan's response to the advent of "revisionism," that fresh and unvarnished look at the structure and exercise of Japanese economic and political power—at Fortress Japan—launched in the late 1980s by journalists James Fallows and Karel van Wolferen, former trade negotiator Clyde Prestowitz, economist Pat Choate, and others inspired in part by the pioneering work of revisionism's intellectual "godfather," political scientist Chalmers Johnson.[3]

Japan wants to be seen as eager to join the rest of the world, but would like to convey this impression while retaining (preferably unperceived) the luxury of its old insular mentality. The revisionists, however, were conducting an extensively researched and persuasively argued critique challenging the longstanding and all-too-convenient conventional wisdom that Japanese institutional arrangements, procedures, motivations, and purposes were fundamentally similar to ours—or at least were unfolding along an American or Western-model trajectory toward free trade, *de facto* parliamentary sovereignty, and more individualistic values. And that if there were still a few glitches of custom and system to be worked out, all that was required was a little more time, patience, and cultural understanding on our part.

This lifting of the silken curtain, with evidence that the revisionist perspectives were beginning to infect the American establishment itself, triggered a panicky Japanese campaign to derail the argument. *Ad hominem* attacks were made on the revisionists as emotional and "unbalanced" in their views, as maladjusted to life in Japan, as racist even. The American conscience was invoked with laments that we were abandoning our grand Ruth Benedict and Margaret Mead tradition of cultural relativism and tolerance for a renascent Puritanical value absolutism. Revisionist ideas were linked to the cruder outbursts of anti-Japanese sentiment in the United States—outbursts that, Tokyo warned, would provoke anti-American feelings in Japan and eventually engulf our own Japanese-American community in yet another round of indignities.

Tokyo's guardians of international reputation and domestic opinion simply will not tolerate on-target (as opposed to cosmetic) criticism of Japan, and they can muster enormous resources against it. As well-established writers enjoying a high profile in Washington, the original revisionists were able to ride out the assault by the Japanese establishment and its American confederates. But the pattern of professional intimidation continues today against other voices with other long-overdue "moments of truth." Americans who study, describe, deal with, and talk to the Japanese must see to it that these precious openings to a true dialogue across the Pacific do not succumb to the ongoing efforts to quash them. We must guarantee that straightforward discussion of Japan (as of China, Russia, or Germany) does not become a political and cultural taboo in our own country.

Prototypical was the case of Karel van Wolferen *prior to* the appearance of his best-selling *The Enigma of Japanese Power* [4] in 1989. A relatively unknown Dutch journalist writing in the spring 1987 issue of *Foreign Affairs*, he found himself roasted by half a dozen nationally prominent figures in a single Japanese opinion journal, with the vendetta continuing on prime-time television. In "The Japan Problem"[5] van Wolferen had suggested that Japan was something less than a free market economy and lacked the effective decision-making center customary for a modern sovereign state. An analysis based on twenty years' reporting from Tokyo, the piece was more judicious than many of the monthly dissections of U.S. economic and social decline that were then appearing in Japan's elite opinion journals. Japan's problem with "The Japan Problem," however, was far less *what* it said—with much of which Japanese officials and scholars privately agreed—than *where* it had been said, namely in the presumed tribune of the American foreign policy establishment.

As one of Japan's business interlocutors put it to me, there was great fear that the notion of a "Japan Problem" would now insinuate itself into the American political mind, much as Peter Drucker's phrase, "adversarial trade," had somehow crawled from the pages of the *Wall Street Journal* into the very text of congressional trade bills.

The May 1987 issue of the conservative opinion journal *Shokun* ran seven individual rebuttals of van Wolferen by a phalanx of national luminaries including former Foreign Minister Saburo Okita; the then Foreign Ministry secretariat chief Hisashi Owada (the father of the girl destined to become Crown Princess Masako); noted political scientist Masataka Kosaka; American Studies authority Nagayo Homma; and Diet member Motoo Shiina, then head of a Japan-U.S. parliamentary exchange group. In tones ranging from deprecatory to derisive, the series hardly got beyond pot-versus-kettle irrelevancies like the U.S. separation of powers, Dutch fumblings on nuclear weapons policy, and the "end of the American Dream."

Not to be outdone by the print media, NHK leapt into the breach with what can only be described as a hostile and manipulative interview of van Wolferen by popular anchorman Hisanori Isomura—at that time perhaps Japan's closest analogue to Walter Cronkite in his prime. With his interviewee no longer present, Isomura concluded with an extended admonition to his captive audience of millions—as a schoolmaster to third-grade pupils—opining that the article had left an unpleasant feeling among Japanese, was too one-sided, and should never have been written at this time when Japan's relations with the U.S. were in a delicate state.

So much for the spirit of free journalism.

Pressures finally were put on van Wolferen's employers when the Japanese ambassador to the Netherlands traveled from The Hague to Rotterdam to lodge a protest with the editors of the daily NRC Handelsblad—who of course had had nothing to do with the *Foreign Affairs* article in the first place. After hearing out the ambassador's solemnly intoned warning that articles like van Wolferen's could hurt the friendship between the

Netherlands and Japan, the editor in chief—his sense of humor much aroused—replied that he did not know how things worked in Japan, but that in his own country they had something known as the freedom of the press. Relations with Japan were an altogether different matter—something the Dutch had chosen to entrust to their government. In any case, the article in an American journal had no connection with his own paper. When it was announced the same week that van Wolferen would be receiving his country's Best Journalist of the Year award for 1986, the Japanese deputy ambassador visited the NRC Handelsblad offices again just to confirm that the prize was *not* being given in recognition of van Wolferen's *Foreign Affairs* piece on Japan. (It was not; it was for his coverage of the ouster of Ferdinand Marcos in the Philippines.)

Since it takes years for a foreign journalist or scholar to develop the personal contacts and entree required to function effectively in Japan's tightly-webbed society, the intimidating design of a coordinated national broadside like this needs little elaboration. In many other instances Foreign Ministry officials have complained to foreign reporters (myself included) or their employers about unflattering articles, which they reflexively condemn for being "biased" or "insufficiently researched." Japanese officials also have an unpleasant habit of accosting foreign correspondents at receptions to question their "motivations" in filing such stories, or to ask if they are perhaps unhappy living in Japan. Since criticism of Japan tends to be taken personally by the Japanese, it is assumed to have a personalized basis on the part of the writer as well.

Even more disturbing has been Japan's reach into the United States itself to intimidate American citizens on their home turf. Given the strength of the Japanese intrusion, the last thing American observers of Japan need is to exercise their own self-censorship. Yet in 1986, Japanese officials joined hands with their American allies in an unsuccessful attempt to bring pressure on the *Atlantic Monthly*'s Washington bureau chief, James Fallows, to tone down the critical thrust of articles he had been writing from Tokyo during a stay there. In a flow of informative and humanly sensitive reports, Fallows had, among other things, recommended "containing" Japan's trade expansion and had etched in sharp relief some of the differences in social values, world view, and educational goals ("Gradgrind's Children") between Japan and his own country.

Fallows had been in East Asia on a fellowship administered by the Japan Society of New York on behalf of the U.S.-Japan Foundation, a private grant-making organization incorporated under U.S. law in 1980 with exclusive funding from Japan's ultra-right-wing Croesus, Ryoichi Sasakawa. As Fallows himself tells the story, he received a letter from an officer of the Japan Society warning that they might have to "reconsider" their relationship with him. He stood his ground, however, and informed his benefactors that as a journalist he had to report things the way he saw them. If this were not possible, he would have to reassess his own relationship with *them*. The Japan Society backed off, but the pressure continued in Tokyo, where a senior Foreign Ministry official, Tatsuo Arima, invited him to lunch for the sole purpose, it seemed, of complaining that his writing was "racist." For a journalist less well established, or one seeking assistance or encomiums from the Japanese, these warnings most likely would have had their intended effect.

More lasting were the blows sustained by Robert Angel, who, unlike the revisionist journalists, had been a political science scholar working *for* the Japanese in the United States. Indeed, he gave them their most potent rhetorical weapon when he coined the term "Japan bashing." Angel, after an enthusiastic start with his employers, eventually concluded that his Washington-based Japan Economic Institute was not conducting the open and disinterested economic research and public discussion he had been led to expect when he accepted its presidency. Increasingly constrained by Japanese embassy dictates, he quit and returned to academic life as the resident Japan policy expert at the University of South Carolina. Continuing his critical analyses of Japan from inside American academe, Angel reports that he has been shunned by the Japanese, cold-shouldered by many of his fellow American Japanologists, and excluded from conferences and dialogues controlled by Japanese spin-doctors and their intellectual amplifiers in the U.S.—now known, in contradistinction to the "Revisionists," as the "Chrysanthemum Club."

Henry Scott Stokes, a British journalist who has spent three decades in Japan, once told me that his loneliest years professionally were those as bureau chief of the *New York Times*, a paper whose presumed political clout in the U.S. impelled many of his long-time Japanese friends to keep a wary distance. Correspondents with less name recognition have had to work up even more courage to write what they think. On 22 July 1994 Victor Fic, a Canadian journalist specializing in defense affairs, received a telephone call from the Foreign Ministry seeking the details of his background, education, area of expertise, and reasons for being interested in Japan. The query, Fic was told, had come from an anonymous reader in Kuala Lumpur who had read two articles of his in the *New Straits Times*, "Japanese Still Denying WWII Truth" (May 14) and "Outside Pressure Needed to Counter Japan's Sinister Right" (July 9). When Fic insisted on knowing the identity of the alleged reader, the Gaimusho hung up and never called back.

From my own experience the questions posed—too labored for a mere Malaysian reader's curiosity—were precisely those the Foreign Ministry starts asking when a foreign journalist becomes sufficiently well-known or problematical, and Fic was probably right in suspecting the hand of a disgruntled Japanese embassy in Kuala Lumpur behind the call. A year earlier, in 1993, the British editor of *PHP Intersect* (a monthly sponsored by the Matsushita group) had apologized for finally rejecting a piece by Fic on Japan's new alien registration law, which had been solicited and rewritten at the editor's request. As Fic wrote me in March 1996, he was informed that "the Japanese co-editors refused to publish it because 'they feel that there is already too much Japan bashing.'"

Finally—in an exercise of censorship that was altogether risible—the conservative *Sankei Shinbun* in October 1995 turned down a submission from one of its regular foreign op-ed contributors. Sheila Johnson (wife of the Japan scholar Chalmers Johnson) had suggested, in a witty send-up of an outmoded 1950s-style U.S. military hotel in Tokyo, that the Security Treaty was now redundant and could be scrapped. Explaining their rejection of her column, the editors of this major national daily solemnly informed Johnson that, after some discussion among themselves, they had decided that U.S.

bases were still needed by Japan, and would she therefore please write on some other topic!

Not much room for a dialogue here, either.

The essential point is that any foreign interlocutor who gets out of line—and does not enjoy the independent leverage of a strong institutional affiliation or an international reputation—is likely to find himself or herself extruded very quickly from the circuit. Foreign scholars of Japan, with their command of the language and their academic standing—always important for the status-minded Japanese—are harder to discredit than the journalistic analysts, but easier to intimidate. Based for the most part at their home universities, Western Japanologists rely on the occasional trip to Japan to garner research materials, conduct interviews, and keep abreast of the work of Japanese experts in their own fields. This practical vulnerability is often intensified by a monkish temperament that eschews public polemics, or by nostalgic memories of earlier residence in Japan as young Ph.D. thesis researchers, when they first intuited that acceptance as a "foreign guest" means not making waves.

It is with foreign academics that we most clearly see how some of the restraints on an open transpacific dialogue are rooted in the very nature of Japanese society itself. To perform his or her own work effectively the typical foreign Japanologist has to join and play the game by Japanese rules that eschew "unacceptable" areas or degrees of criticism. Going along risks intellectual (and ethical) emasculation through self-censorship, while breaking the rules invites banishment—not much of a choice. In a 1985 speech at the International House of Japan in Tokyo, Glen S. Fukushima, then with the Office of the United States Trade Representative, noted the "strange propensity among American Japanologists to feel one-sidedly positive about Japan." This, he said, was because, "if you're a foreigner who is too critical about Japan, your sources of information, funding, or friends dry up."[6] How true. Japan's collectivist social groupings, with their all-or-nothing emotional bonding, cannot accommodate the sort of dry matter-of-fact dissent that in most other societies does not threaten basic loyalties or friendships. Access in Japan depends excessively on a warm personal rapport, for the sake of which too many American scholars, cultural diplomats, and other intellectuals with a stake in Japan have trimmed their critical sails.

I myself can authenticate these hazards from personal experience, since I have written very openly in the media of both countries ever since 1986–1987 about the problems of "academic apartheid" and other aspects of Japanese intellectual insularity and cultural nationalism—in the *Wall Street Journal, Washington Post, Los Angeles Times,* and the *National Interest,* and in Japanese in the *Chuo Koron, Ronza,* and numerous op-ed columns for the *Sankei Shinbun* where I have been hitched to the same "stable" of foreign writers as Sheila Johnson since 1988.[7] For those foreigners willing to bear a certain personal cost, however, I must stress the importance and feasibility of speaking out.

Actually, you can count on considerable sympathy and intellectual agreement from your Japanese friends in most walks of life. Your notoriety, as Karel van Wolferen soon found out, can even serve to open new doors for you. The brush-off comes, rather, from those scholars and government officials among your professional and social acquaintances appointed (or self-appointed) to monitor and guide the intellectual flow across the Pacific through their influence on fellowships, conference invitations, university appointments, and the Tokyo-Washington gossip grapevine. In 1994 I learned that highly placed Japanese on that nexus were writing off my published views as "sour grapes," following my legal proceedings against a Japanese university in 1993, as briefly noted in Chapter 1. It was a typical *ad hominem* ploy, and one that stood the chronology on its head, since I had already been writing in a similar vein for seven years. Indeed, in 1990 one of Japan's younger ambassadors, whom I had known earlier as a friend in Washington but who was then in charge of his ministry's foreign press relations, walked up to me at a Japan National Press Club reception just long enough to mutter, "Hall-san, you are a bad influence on American journalists!" The ambassador, Taizo Watanabe, once shared lodgings at the Yale graduate school with a former Princeton undergraduate roommate of mine, and he had been one of my contacts for Friendship Commission business at the

Japanese embassy in Washington. So much for former personal and professional ties.

What stuck in Japan's establishmentarian craw was the way I had moved beyond that sort of euphemistic criticism that roundly deplores effects—to a chorus of painless *mea culpas* from one's Japanese readers—to search for causes in the more sensitive and possibly embarassing areas of political will, national goals, insular mentality, and plain racial prejudice. My own nuisance value to the Japanese, however, has never merited more than a swat or two (unless this book changes that). Indeed, the more pernicious put-downs often come from fellow foreigners who urge upon you a greater timidity and circumspection, if they have not already dismissed you altogether as a "Japan basher."

In October 1987, I was invited to a luncheon meeting of the Tokyo Political Officers Club, an informal gathering of political attachés, to elaborate on my 6 July 1987, *Wall Street Journal* op-ed piece, "Stop Making Excuses for Japan's Insularity." As the session broke up, a quietly fuming diplomat from a major Latin American country confided to me, "I agree with you 300 percent, it bears out my entire experience here." Apart from a sympathetic defense of Japan's "cultural uniqueness" from a South Asian diplomat whose nation had never been occupied by the Japanese army, the only dissent came from the young political attaché of a small landlocked European country. His alarm over my article was so great that he preferred to convey it to me later in the privacy of a luncheon for two. At an elegant French restaurant he told me that he could not agree more with my analysis, but that it was a great mistake to have gone public with it. That would only drive the Japanese more deeply into their shell. My views would have been more effective, he sermonized, had I conveyed them discreetly to a few highly placed Japanese. I was appalled by the young man's naiveté. His embassy had little political business with Japan, and with time on his hands he had been devoting himself with commendable earnestness to the study of Japanese language and culture. He admitted, however, that the economic staff of his embassy probably saw things my way.

How wrong my diplomat friend had been was suggested by my presentation of very similar points in one of my *Sankei* columns the following year. A month later in the same space, in a piece lambasting the "self-centeredness" that had brought so much foreign pressure to bear on Japan, a former Japanese ambassador to West Germany, Akira Sono, picked up my toughest phrase to remark approvingly:

> The egoistic spirit of the Japanese people was concretely criticized in this column by Ivan Hall, visiting professor at Keio University. I have been active overseas many years as a diplomat, and there are many points of resemblance between Mr. Hall's view of Japan and mine. In particular, his remark that, "It is the already existing Japanese protectionism which has provoked the threat of American protectionism," really hits the nail on the head.[8]

Foreign outspokenness, far from driving the Japanese further into their shell, often can have the opposite effect of emboldening those—a considerable "silent minority"—who have critical views of their own country but are reluctant to commit themselves against a powerful domestic consensus unless they have some foreign props to lean on. Since it is difficult to criticize Japan from the inside without being considered disloyal or even un-Japanese, nothing is more destructive of such fledgling civic courage than the gratuitous, patronizing, and injudicious reconfirmation of Japan's insular nationalism by foreign political or intellectual authorities. We simply must learn to talk straight to the Japanese, in a firm but friendly fashion, with neither bluster nor squishy self-abnegation.

I can still recall the way an eminent British Japanologist reddened visibly under the ears as he glanced through my *Wall Street Journal* piece in the bustling lobby of the International House of Japan—that Grand Central Station of globe-trotting foreign scholars. The problem, he retorted after scanning it, was that the nations of Europe and America were still refusing to admit Japan into the "White Man's Club." Try selling that, I thought, to the U.S. or E.U. trade negotiators!

THE MERETRICIOUS PROMISE OF "KOKUSAIKA"

Japan's insular mentality is, I believe, the ultimate source of most of its difficulties with other countries. Accordingly, for our part we need urgently to comprehend that Japan does *not* plan to become more open or cosmopolitan in the way Americans and others suppose when they hear Japanese spokesmen say that their country is determined to "internationalize"—something we assume to be a condition for regional, let alone global, leadership going into the twenty-first century. Their feeling of separateness has led the Japanese to definitions and practical approaches to "opening up" that are very different from our own understanding of the matter. Japan's promised "internationalization," known as *kokusaika*, is indeed more a device for continued anxious self-protection than for a fresh outward engagement with the rest of the world.

What we are dealing with here is, strictly speaking, the current attenuated residue of Japan's long bout with insular ideology. In its full viral strength, as it developed out of Shinto nationalism in the eighteenth century, it lodged itself in the Imperial ideology of the Meiji Constitution, and came to full flower in the 1930s with the official cultural-nationalist tract *Kokutai no Hongi* (Fundamental Principles of the National Polity)[9] and the super-insularism of a Greater East Asia Coprosperity Sphere orchestrated by Japan. Nevertheless, the slogan *kokusaika* encodes Japanese interpretations of "internationalization" that are profoundly anti-cosmopolitan.

For two decades now we have heard *kokusaika* chanted as though it were a totem that by itself would somehow turn the trick. The "International Hotel" in a provincial town that would go into shock if a real foreigner ever were to walk through the door represents a harmless fad similar to that of the sobriquet "imperial" a century ago. A more insidious distortion lies in the flaunting of what we might call international chic—the conspicuous display of German luxury automobiles and Parisian haute couture; the jetting off to international conferences at Maui or Talloires; the showy use of English in front of one's monolingual countrymen; or the fashion for Christian-style weddings for non-Christian couples, who nod solemn assent to the unfamiliar injunctions of St. Paul as their aunts and uncles stumble bravely through the canned hymns. Such activities are mistaken by their practitioners for genuine "internationalization," while they give the term itself a bad name among ordinary Japanese.

The type of *kokusaika* envisioned by most Japanese is one that ranks them high on the scale of cosmopolitanism as they define it, while ignoring the dimension of greatest concern to others. Fearing the contamination of their own social structures by live foreign participation, the Japanese continue to promote "internationalization"—as they did *kaikoku* or "opening the country" in the Meiji era—as a matter of things as opposed to people, a prodigious effort to admit foreign civilization at the material, institutional, and intellectual levels, but never foreign people. "Things" over the past century have included the entire gamut of Western artifacts from Manchester-built locomotives in the 1890s to MacDonald's hamburgers in the 1990s, the adaptation of entire legal and educational systems, the mastery of foreign arts and technologies from playing Beethoven to flying jets, the appropriation of Western thought from Jesus to Marx to Milton Friedman, the learning of European languages, the translation of everything under the sun, and the earnest study and appreciation of other civilizations and cultures. Now, the Japanese contend, it is time for others to master their tongue, to study their national history, and learn to savor the subtle flavors of sushi. And they are right, as far as "things" go.

The downside of this formula is that it deliberately minimizes human contact—the pattern first set by the Meiji government when it sent students abroad and invited foreign teachers to Japan, putting each of the two groups back on the return steamer just as quickly as possible. This is not the sort of "internationalization" most of the outside world expects today, as Japan's partners seek access by their own nationals to institutions and activities—commercial, legal, journalistic, and academic—that have a direct impact on Japanese as well as on international affairs.

It is indeed striking how Japanese cultural commentators and exchange experts continue to insist that the professional barriers to foreigners today are of a culturally determined and therefore virtually intractable nature, rather than the product of specific ordinances and historical decisions of relatively recent provenance and consequently reversible, given enough political will and courage. Underlying it all is the usually unspoken fear that opening Japan to fuller participation by foreign people would destroy Japanese identity itself, the way a clam dies once it has been pried open. In 1987, a leading national daily conducted a study of public reactions to the growing foreign criticism of Japan's closed market and society and found voices here and there willing to accept limitations on Japanese exports and to endure a lowered standard of living, if a policy of "moderate seclusionism" were required to stop foreigners from trying to impose their own "attitudes toward life" and "beliefs" on Japan.[10]

Japan's concept of "internationalization" as a controlled ingestion of foreign civilization while keeping foreigners themselves at bay, rests on a perception of racial and cultural homogeneity as something that is both dynamically creative and easily destroyed. This stands in sharp contrast to the American article of faith that human diversity is invariably a source of national creativity and strength. Calls for *kokusaika* from the late 1970s were often bracketed with admonitions to get a firm handle on Japanese identity first. At Tsukuba National University when I taught there in the mid-1980s, the new emphases on foreign language training and area studies—under the banner of *kokusaika* —seemed directed less at a broad intellectual cosmopolitanism than at preparing young combatants for the trade wars, both overseas and in coping with the problems created by market liberalization at home. In the new department of Japanese Language and Culture created for the laudable purpose of turning out graduates who could serve in Japan's long-overdue language and cultural programs abroad, some students told me they were worried about being plied with too precise definitions of what Japanese culture actually *was*—a regression, in other words, to the official defining that went on in the prewar educational system, when Japanese citizens were incessantly being told by their own rulers *who* they were.

Cultural nationalism as an ideological force reemerged with the economic successes of the 1970s and 1980s, taking the form of a preoccupation with so-called *nihonjinron* (theories about the Japanese). It no longer touts the divine origin of the Japanese race descended from the Sun Goddess, the mystical unity of the people with their emperor, or the sacred singularity of the national polity, the main buttresses of the official ideology up to

1945. It retains, however, the core notion of uniqueness, which similarly permeates Japanese formulations of *kokusaika*. A cottage industry of *nihonjinron* writing by some of Japan's leading scholars as well as freelance hacks flourishes to supply the seemingly insatiable appetite of the Japanese public for what makes them different from others. There is, they are reassured, a spiritual dimension to the Japanese language—language being the bedrock of any national culture—which is beyond the ken of non-Japanese no matter how fluent they become. The Japanese brain itself is different, managing to process harmoniously both thought and feeling in the left hemisphere, whereas *all other* peoples have to make do with split wiring—aesthetics and emotions in the right lobe, logical thinking in the left. There are communal harmonies, the end-product of a long trajectory of autogenic and impermeable cultural development, that account for Japan's spectacular economic performance and render the superficially transplanted institutions of modern law and political democracy less critical for the good society than is the case in the West. Japanese remove their overcoats before entering a host's home, Americans after crossing the threshhold, and that—like everything else—has some ineffable bearing on trade disputes, the unfortunate result of the failure by others to appreciate all of the above.[11]

Culture, in short, lies in the blood, and that is why—though left unspoken—a genuine *kokusaika* of peoples, a real dismantling of Japan's cartels of the mind, could never seriously be entertained. It is not hard to imagine the deadening hand this ideology of self-protective uniqueness placed on personal encounters and cultural exchange activities as actual contacts with foreigners grew steadily after 1970. Even more than the treatment of thoroughly acculturated resident Koreans, the true touchstone of Japan's sense of inviolate purity has been its continued shunning of the *burakumin* "outcastes" who are physically and culturally indistinguishable from other Japanese—or the flight of Japan's AIDS sufferers, rejected by their own families, who die in hospices abroad.[12] As with all purists, 98 percent conformity can be more threatening than outright deviation.

Negative feelings towards blacks have also been allowed to

erupt openly from time to time, causing avoidable political difficulties with Japan's major partner, as when Prime Minister Nakasone in 1986 publicly denigrated the intelligence of American blacks and Hispanics. The hand of racial prejudice against Caucasians has been stayed simply by the power relationship with the West and not by any intrinsic liking for whites—a point usually lost on Tokyo's Beautiful Pale-faced People, those transient representatives of Western economic, political, and military clout.

The cost of this insularity to Japan's cultural diplomacy was most poignantly suggested to me by two of India's leading artistic and scholarly figures, one of them the world-renowned founder of one of India's leading dance companies. He once confided to me, in the presence of the Indian ambassador to Tokyo, that, whereas a few minutes' shop talk with his counterparts in Europe or the Americas usually sufficed to establish an open personal rapport based on mutual professional interests, he had never gotten to first base with his Japanese peers, despite years of visiting lectureships in Japan. The other was a historian from New Delhi who, with a graceful laugh to match her elegantly bright sari, told a roomful of somberly suited Japanese scholars at a Tokyo conference on the Meiji Restoration that they should be less fearful of outside influences, citing India's hospitable absorption over the centuries of wave after breaking wave of foreign civilization. As Hindus these two Indians were heirs to Asia's most ancient tradition, whereas I came from an almost antipodal culture. But we had at times run up against identical personal and intellectual walls with the Japanese.

The sheer physical root of the we/they consciousness toward non-Japanese was most poignantly exposed by the AIDS scare that first surfaced in the mid-1980s, when one looked in vain for a public sense that a common human tragedy and challenge was at hand. From the initial reactions one would have judged that the plague had been carried in exclusively by external agents—by tainted plasma from America, by foreign sailors alighting at the Kobe docks, by visiting gays from Castro Street. To some paranoid Japanese, a white or black face was enough to suggest the dread disease, but as foreign lechers were turned away from the local citadels of sin no one thought to plug or even mention the biggest leak in the whole boat—those massive sex-tour migrations of Japanese men to the neighboring fleshpots of Asia. Once again, at the time of the great Hanshin (Osaka-Kobe) earthquake in January 1995, Japan surprised the world by delaying or declining the services of French doctors, Swiss avalanche dogs, American hospital ships, and other outside assistance—ostensibly because of bureaucratic quibbles, but leaving the impression that outsiders were not really welcome and that Japan did not want to be seen as needing help.

The truth of the matter is that the Japanese simply do not want non-Japanese physically present among them for any length of time, embedded as individuals in the working institutions of their society. As short-term feted guests or curiosities, yes; but not as fixed human furniture. Permanent intrusions are viewed by the Japanese as intolerable threats to their value system, their social relationships, their way of life. Market access, too, is ultimately feared less for its purely economic impact than as the opening wedge for a greater foreign social presence in Japan. A truly open market, after all, would bring in not only more foreign goods but more foreign business people, lawyers, and laborers who would spill out of the narrow enclosures that have successfully contained them for over a century and invade the mainstream of Japanese life.

What has been missing from Japan's historical conceptualization of itself in respect to both the West and Asia is a capacity to think in terms of "horizontal" relationships among equals—a greater sensitivity to universal human traits and needs and interests, overriding the rigid verticalities of superior-inferior power relationships and the precipitous intercultural chasms that still dominate the Japanese view of the outside world. Having climbed to the top of the pile, Japan has difficulty deciding where to go next, since it cannot imagine simply going sideways—toward a relaxed collegiality.

In short, what prevents Japan's assumption of an enlightened world leadership role is, more than anything else, its overblown particularism. Great powers in human history have all predicated their mandate (however presumptuous or self-serving) on some sort of universalism. That goes for the great imperial purveyors of political *pax*—be it America, Britain, ancient Rome, or even the perverted communist universalism of the old Soviet bloc—as well as for the major cultural players like France, with its self-appointed *mission civilisatrice*, and the Chinese with their superb self-confidence over the ages that the barbarians at the gates would eventually succumb to the overpowering charm of Chinese culture.

Indeed, one of the most striking features of contemporary, hi-tech Japan is the persistent Japanese fear of the adoption of their own culture by others, an attitude that contrasts most starkly with that of the French. A foreigner in France who does not know the language, or handles it poorly, has traditionally been *persona non grata*—precisely the reverse of Japan, where the fluent foreigner seems threatening and intrusive, and the complete linguistic and cultural ingenue is welcomed with open arms and sighs of relief. In France a reasonable mastery of the French language and culture by a resident foreign artist, scholar, or journalist usually leads to professional and personal treatment no worse than that which Frenchmen accord one another. In Japan anxiety over the acculturation of others to their culture—together with the conviction that it simply cannot be done—leads most Japanese to view the effort less as a compliment or first step toward bonding than as an unwanted prying into their national psyche.

Unfortunately, the evidence to date suggests the difficulty of convincing the Japanese that their great influence in the world today makes reciprocal access to their society all but mandatory. Most, instead, when pressed, will elevate their exclusionism to a cultural principle requiring tolerance and acceptance by others on the basis of cultural relativism. True reciprocity, in other words, means Japanese respect for American openness, and American respect for Japanese exclusivity. The demands for intellectual access represent Western absolutes, a new form of cultural imperialism. Heads I win, tails you lose. The economic and political implications of this insular rubric are mind-boggling, but that is the bottom line of Japan's repeated pledges of "internationalization."

Conclusion

WAKE-UP CALL: Let the Daylight In

On a midnight talk show on Nihon Television on 25–26 December 1994, policy pundit Kenichi Ohmae opined, to the consenting nods of his fellow panelists, that Japan might be entering a period of *shin sakoku*, that is to say, a "new seclusion." The term *sakoku* normally refers to the self-imposed "closing of the country" under the Tokugawa shogunate, but Ohmae was reflecting on what he saw as a growing lack of interest among ordinary Japanese in international affairs. A number of foreigners in Japan in the mid-1990s, myself included, have begun asking whether the country may not indeed be heading for a sort of Heisei Sakoku ("Heisei" being the present Emperor's era-name). The closing would come in subtle ways of the mind and spirit, but at a very high level of affluence, technological sophistication, and carefully managed ties so as not to impair Japan's economic access to world markets.

Meanwhile, as American branch campuses in Japan collapse ignominiously and as American scholars are unceremoniously dismissed from Japan's national and private universities, Japan continues to send its professors to Berkeley and Chicago, its bureaucrats to the Kennedy School at Harvard, its engineers to Caltech and MIT, its hospital interns to Massachusetts General and its medical researchers to NIH, its camera-makers to Rochester, its journalist trainees to Missouri or Columbia, and its correspondents to every press conference and news event in Washington that they have the inclination and energy to cover. In asking the Japanese to dismantle their cartels of the mind, nothing is so effective for starters as sheer exposure. The vested interests these structures serve and the fortress mentality that sustains them must first be driven from the shadows of anonymity, where they feed and luxuriate on the assumption that the outside world doesn't know, or, if it did, wouldn't care. Names must be named, and protest systematically sustained, yet the mid-1990s finds the foreigners' energies close to exhaustion in pursuing those issues.

Japan's leaders, then, need to be given convincing evidence that others do indeed see their intellectual barriers for the protectionist anachronisms that they are. Their country's leadership in the world outside can only come from more relaxed internal postures toward it. If the Japanese really aspire to becoming a "normal country," they must learn to create in their own society the openness that has enabled them to benefit so abundantly from the markets, knowledge, and human contact that have been made available to them throughout the world. A dynamic global power practicing both economic and intellectual mercantilism will be increasingly awkward to accommodate. Indeed, as high costs and regulatory barriers increasingly impel foreign firms and media organizations to move their regional headquarters to alternative sites like Singapore or Hong Kong (despite its absorption by a communist state), Tokyo risks forfeiting to the more cosmopolitan Chinese its ambition to become the financial and informational hub of a newly booming Asia.

This does not mean that the Japanese have to love or like non-Japanese—any more than the openness of others has meant loving or liking them. Compatibility, let alone intimacy, operate on a different plane from functional access—the sort of access for non-nationals that the Japanese have been accorded elsewhere. At the very least, the Japanese will have to develop a greater sensitivity to the economic or social harm they occasionally inflict on others. They will have to learn to take compromises and adjustments in their stride as the normal

condition of an interdependent world rather than as concessions to outside pressure, to be made as slowly and grudgingly
as possible. Our own goal should be the emergence of a frank
and untrammelled dialogue across the Pacific similar in every
way to that which spans the Atlantic. That, of course, would by
its very nature threaten Japan's mental insularity, and our
pursuit of it is bound to meet with a great deal of resistance. All
the more reason, then, to get on with it.

For the American side I hesitate to present specific recommendations here that should be fairly obvious from the preceding
chapters. They are in any case destined to be ignored unless and
until the United States abandons its rigid laissez-faire trade ideology and sets itself to a comprehensive economic, political, and
intellectual engagement with East Asia for the long run.
But let us briefly conjure with half a dozen basic desiderata:

1. Wouldn't it be nice, for example, if the various national
   associations for the American legal, media, and academic
   professions—together with our diplomats and those Americans immediately affected in Tokyo—were to present a
   united front, committed for the long term, pressing for
   equal access in Japan? Confronted with that tsunami of
   international disapproval, Tokyo might simply be shamed
   into taking at least the minimally acceptable measures.
   These would include allowing foreign lawyers to hire
   Japanese partners and associates; permitting every
   accredited foreign correspondent to attend all on-the-record
   press conferences; and extending full collegial treatment to
   foreign professors—the essential privileges that Japanese
   lawyers, journalists, and scholars enjoy in the United States.
2. Since the formal restrictions on foreign teachers,
   researchers, and students are decreed by what has often
   been called Japan's most conservative central ministry—
   one ruled by bureaucrats with minimal scholarly empathies
   or credentials—nothing short of high, multilateral, and
   continued diplomatic pressure is likely to bring significant
   changes here. Indeed, Japanese universities are not likely to
   generate any meaningful *kokusaika* unless they are freed

from a variety of direct and indirect Monbusho controls and receive their national funding through an autonomous body such as Britain's pre-1989 University Grants Committee.

3. Federal agencies specifically entrusted with the nurturing of American intellectual ties with Japan such as the Japan-U.S. Friendship Commission, the U.S. Information Agency, and the National Science Foundation should deal forthrightly with these egregious barriers to reciprocity. Considering all that it has done to open the United States to Japanese culture in the past, the bilateral CULCON should be terminated if the Japanese side refuses even to discuss the lowering of legal and regulatory barriers faced by American students and scholars in Japan.

4. Americans should be less squeamish about taking their own compensatory measures, particularly where they frequently have been suggested as in the case of the kisha clubs. As with economic sanctions, however, we need to drop the language of "retaliation" or "containment," terms that alienate nonconfrontational Americans and play to Japan's sense of victimization. The United States has, from John K. Galbraith's study of *American Capitalism* in 1952 and from its early twentieth-century experience in curbing the excessive "private power" of big business and big labor, a splendidly serviceable concept for dealing with Japan's economic and intellectual cartels—that of *countervailing* actions, or "countervailing power."

5. Americans active in the transpacific dialogue should at least be aware of the manipulative tactics of veiling and intimidation that I discussed in the last chapter. For those who agree with Japan's positions, well and good, but there should be a national consensus that no one is to be sidelined from a free and open debate. Those who don't agree with Tokyo should come better prepared with the full range of rebuttals. By the same token, our intellectuals at home should not be afraid to express negative judgments in public or in print—the only way to persuade the Japanese that we really mean what we say—for fear of losing an entree for research, one's position as a "cultural bridger,"

or perhaps even a chance at a diplomatic posting to Tokyo. The American public would have a good laugh if it could envision all the ambassadorial sugarplums that dance in Japan scholars' heads during a presidential election year.

6. Finally, the last thing the United States should do—for its own sake, and for that of Japanese democracy—is to demand or accept a larger Japanese military contribution to the American strategic position in East Asia as a satisfactory substitute for the economic and social opening of Japan.

The problems laid out in this book, like the broader tapestry of Japan itself, remain extremely remote from everyday working-stiff America, including all but a tiny fraction of its "chattering classes." The heaviest responsibility, therefore, devolves on those American intellectuals who have assigned themselves an interlocutory role in our relations with Japan— particularly those who have been embraced by Japan's cultural, business, and political establishments.

Those Japan scholars who have made too much of a good thing out of cultural sensitivity in deferring to Japan's insularity should bear in mind that their own interposition in the public affairs of two great powers is an anomaly in the wider world, a seductive opportunity created by the very limited number of fellow citizens familiar with Japan and its language. By way of contrast the distinguished American scholar of Milton or Disraeli who visits England is likely to spend long hours at the British Museum and find his or her chief diversion in the ale and pork pie served at the pubs outside the gate—not in the parliamentary chambers at Westminster or at receptions of the Federation of British Industries. Even in our more complicated relations with the Germans, America's leading Germanists, Bonn correspondents, and analysts of the Federal Republic's economy, do not presume to broker the broader relationship between the two peoples. In a word, America's Japan hands should worry less about protecting their own role on the playing field of Japan-U.S. power politics, and get back to doing what they of all people can do best—calling the shots exactly as they see them.

I am not sanguine about any sudden surge of tough-mindedness in the U.S. Few of the American go-betweens—based for the most part on home soil and enjoying the considerable perks of noncontroversial go-betweening—have ever had to buck Japan's cartels of the mind directly in Japan. Too many Americans remain caught in our dominant assumption since the 1950s—most clearly enunciated by our succession of paternalistic ambassadors to Tokyo from Edwin Reischauer in the 1960s to Mike Mansfield in the 1980s—that the Japanese are gradually converging toward our own institutions and values, and that too much complaining might throw them off track and slip the security knot. For over a century Europe and America have swung between giantizing and trivializing Japan, and few Westerners today have a judicious grasp of the new nationalism and growing Asian orientation that are likely to keep Japan's intellectual barriers firmly in place. But all this leads us away from Japan's cartels of the mind toward an exploration of our own American mind on Japan. And that requires another kind of treatment, perhaps in another book.

Notes

Introduction

1. I am indebted for this expression to Chalmers A. Johnson, who used it in the title of his article, "Artificial Cartels of the Mind Justify Distrust of Japan," *International Herald Tribune*, 16 June 1993.

2. This phrase was launched by conservative opposition leader Ichiro Ozawa in his international attention-getter, *Blueprint for a New Japan: The Rethinking of a Nation*, Tokyo, Kodansha International, 1994; translated from the Japanese original, *Nihon Kaizo Keikaku* (Plan for the Restructuring of Japan), Tokyo, Kodansha, 1993.

3. Edward Seidensticker, *This Country Japan*, Tokyo, Kodansha, 1984, p. 332.

4. James Sterngold, "A Hard Lesson on Trade for Mondale," *New York Times*, 20 February 1994.

5. Teresa Watanabe, "Mondale Quickly Learned the Ways of the Japanese," from the *Los Angeles Times* as carried in the *Daily Yomiuri*, 10 November 1996.

1 LEGAL LANDING: THE ATTORNEYS' NARROW BEACHHEAD

1. Yoshio Suzuki, *Nihon no Shiho, Koko ga Mondai: Bengoshi Kaizo Keikaku* (Japan's Judicial System, Here's the Problem: The Restructuring Plan for Lawyers), Tokyo, Toyo Keizai Shinposha, 1991. Suzuki, who has served on prestigious committees for administrative reform, focuses on the long and as yet futile attempt to persuade the *bengoshi* (a limited elite of litigation lawyers) to permit a significant expansion of their profession, and touches on the "price cartel."

2. Shingo Miyake, *Bengoshi Karuteru: Girudo-ka suru "Zaiya" Hoso no Jitsuzo* (Lawyers' Cartel: The True Image of Our "Non-Establishment" Legal Profession that Is Becoming a Guild), Tokyo, Shinzansha Shuppan, 1995. Miyake, a Columbia-trained legal affairs editor for the *Nihon Keizai Shinbun*, concentrates on the antitrust aspects of the minimum-fee schedules, with useful updates on the British, French, and German legal professions.

3. For a richly informative description of Japan's legal professionals see Robert Brown, "A Lawyer by Any Other Name: Legal Advisors in Japan," a book-length survey that appears as Chapter 8 in Edward J. Lincoln and Douglas E. Rosenthal, Chairmen, *Legal Aspects of Doing Business in Japan, 1983*, Commercial Law and Practice Course Handbook Series No. 295, New York, Practicing Law Institute, 1983, pp. 201–502. My statistics in these paragraphs have for the most part been drawn from Suzuki, *Nihon no Shiho*, and from Yasuo Watanabe et al., *Tekisutobukku Gendai Shiho* (Textbook: The Modern Judicial System), 2d ed., Tokyo, Nihon Hyoronsha, 1994. For my general treatment of the *bengoshi* I am also indebted to: Charles R. Stevens, "Japanese Law and the Japanese Legal System: Perspectives for the American Business Lawyer," *The Business Lawyer*, Vol. 27, No. 4, July 1972; Stephen Clayton, "More Lawyers than Meet the Eye," *PHP*, November 1984; Chapter 5 in John Owen Haley, *Authority without Power: Law and the Japanese Paradox*, New York and Oxford, Oxford University Press, 1991; and briefer treatments in articles from Tokyo's English-language press.

4. For the EPA's comparison see *Nikkei Weekly*, 19 July 1993.

5. This critical point was persuasively developed by Robert F. Grondine, chairman of the legal services committee of the American Chamber of Commerce in Japan, in "Layers of Lawyers," *Business Tokyo*, March 1988. For the development of the foreign lawyers' access issue I have relied on the articles and documents cited below for quotation, on a variety of press clippings, and on an interview and materials kindly provided by Mr. Grondine on 2 March 1995.

6. Leonardo Ciano, "Japan's Changes to Its Foreign Lawyer Law: Black Ships Revisited or Did Someone Miss the Boat?" in *Hosei Riron* (Legal Theory), Vol. 27, No. 1, August 1994, p. 22. This is the most comprehensive technical treatment of the *gaiben* question, by a young Canadian lawyer and legal scholar currently teaching in Japan.

7. Karen Dillon, "Unfair Trade?" in *The American Lawyer*, April 1994, p. 56.

8. Ciano, "Japan's Changes to Its Foreign Lawyer Law," p. 39.

9. Junjiro Tsubota, "Law Suits and Legal Consciousness," *PHP*, November 1984, pp. 29, 27.

10. "*Bengoshi wa, kihonteki jinken o hogo shi, shakai seigi o jitsugen suru koto o shimei to suru.*" Watanabe et al., *Gendai Shiho*, p. 114.

11. As reported by Rieko Nakao, "Foreign Lawyers Grab Slim Toehold in Japan," *Daily Yomiuri*, 26 June 1987.

12. Suzuki, *Nihon no Shiho*, p. 38.

13. Akira Kawamura, "Justice for All," *Japan Scope*, Autumn 1994, p. 69.

14. *Ibid.*, p. 70.

15. Richard A. Cole, "A *Gaiben* Invasion?" in *Tokyo Business Today*, April 1992, p. 49.

16. Report carried in *Japan Scope*, Autumn 1994, p. 63.

17. Personal interview with Robert F. Grondine in Tokyo, 2 March 1995.

18. Robert F. Grondine, in his Statement for the American Bar Association and the American Chamber of Commerce in Japan Legal Services Committee, delivered before the JFBA on 1 April 1993; and in "Foreign Law Firms in Japan Thwarted," *International Financial Law Review*, July 1994, pp. 12, 15.

19. Eamonn Fingleton, *Blindside: Why Japan Is Still on Track to Overtake the U.S. by the Year 2000*, New York, Houghton Mifflin Co., 1995, pp. 54–55, 62. J. Mark Ramseyer, "Lawyers, Foreign Lawyers, and Lawyers-Substitute: The Market for Regulation in Japan," *Harvard International Law Journal*, Special Issue, Vol. 27, 1986, pp. 499–539.

20. Bruce Rutledge, "Seeing It from All Sides: Breaking into Japan's Legal Markets," *Japan Scope*, Autumn 1994, p. 62.

21. Grondine, statement before the JFBA on 1 April 1993.

22. Stephen Clayton, "More Lawyers than Meet the Eye," pp. 13–14.

23. Chalmers Johnson, "Artificial Cartels of the Mind Justify Distrust of Japan," *International Herald Tribune*, 16 June 1993.

24. Bob Deans, "Patience Pays Off for American Attorney in Japan," *Asahi Evening News*, 17 August 1988.

25. As reported by Cameron Hay, *Japan Times*, 1 January 1993.

26. *Asahi Evening News*, 13 April 1993.

27. Editorial in *Nikkei Weekly*, the English-language digest of the *Nihon Keizai Shinbun*, 11 October 1993.

28. *Nikkei Weekly*, 19 July 1993.

29. Cole, "A *Gaiben* Invasion?" p. 49.

30. Ciano, "Japan's Changes to Its Foreign Lawyer Law," p. 15.

31. E. Anthony Zaloom, "An American Lawyer Comes to Japan," *Japan Quarterly*, January–March 1988, p. 51.

32. Karen Dillon, "Unfair Trade?" pp. 55–56.

2 SEGREGATED SCRIBES:
THE FOREIGN CORRESPONDENTS

1. For the events described in this chapter I have drawn on the following: (a) the cornucopia of ongoing coverage preserved in the clipping files of the library of the Foreign Correspondents' Club of Japan (FCCJ), including the English-language press in Tokyo with occasional material from the Japanese press and from English-language media abroad; (b) the running account of the kisha club problem since 1968 in the monthly issues of the *No.1 Shimbun*, the journal of the FCCJ; (c) the official minutes of the Foreign Press in Japan (FPIJ) since 1959, also available at the FCCJ; (d) other sources mentioned in the following footnotes; and (e) my own experience as the accredited Tokyo correspondent for the *Philadelphia Bulletin* and *Washington Star* from 1970 to 1976, and as a professional associate member of the FCCJ since 1977. Footnote references have been confined to quotations, special sources, and points of exceptional note.

2. "2 US Reporters Storm 'Kisha Club,'" *Mainichi Daily News*, 22 May 1993.

3. Michael Shari, "Financial News Wires Face 'High Wall to Lucrative Sources,'" *Nikkei Weekly*, 2 November 1992.

4. "2 US Reporters," *Mainichi Daily News*, 22 May 1993.

5. Thomas Boatman, "A Foreigner's Crusade for a Free Press in Japan," *Asahi Evening News*, 25 September 1994.

6. Robert Whiting, "Prying Open Japan's Press Clubs," *Tokyo Journal*, November 1986, p. 11.

7. Kazue Suzuki, *The Press Club System in Japan*, a master's thesis submitted to Iowa State University, Ames, Iowa, 1982, p. 36. This very useful study is the sole book-length treatment of the kisha clubs in any language. I have drawn the historical background in these two paragraphs from the copy donated by the author to the Foreign Correspondents' Club of Japan.

8. The quotes and the account in this paragraph are from Chapter 11 of Frank Kelley and Cornelius Ryan, *Star Spangled Mikado*, New York, R. M. McBride, 1947, serialized in *No.1 Shimbun*, January–March 1994. The name of FCCJ's in-house journal derives not from the hubris of the fourth estate but from the address informally bestowed on the original club building at "#1 Shimbun Alley, Tokyo." The journal still uses the older romanization *shimbun* for "newspaper," rather than the now standard *shinbun*.

9. "Club Prexy Urges Freer Flow of News," *No.1 Shimbun*, October 1968.

10. "Ugo Asks Japan Press to Remove News Obstacles," *No.1 Shimbun*, October 1969.

11. "Chrysler Speaks," *No.1 Shimbun*, October 1972.

12. Quotes from letter from the Nihon Shinbun Kyokai to the International Press Institute, Zurich, autumn of 1968, reprinted ("Shimbun Kyokai for the Defense") in *No.1 Shimbun*, December 1968. My own emphasis in italics.

13. From the *Shinbun Kyokaiho*, 15 October 1968, as translated by Ken Ishii, chairman of the FPIJ, in *No.1 Shimbun*, December 1968.

14. Don Oberdorfer, "Conferring Editors Probe Access," *No.1 Shimbun*, October 1973.

15. Translation provided by *Mainichi Daily News* and carried as "Ex-Spokesman Strikes Back," *No.1 Shimbun*, October 1973.

16. Donald Kirk, "Press Club Door Opens—a Bit," *No.1 Shimbun*, May, 1974.

17. Sonia Katchian, "Japanese Kisha Clubs Present Problems For Photographers Too," *No.1 Shimbun*, February 1988.

18. Robert Whiting, "Prying Open Japan's Press Clubs," p. 12.

19. "An Open Letter from Foreign Correspondents in Japan," *Mainichi Daily News*, 22 April 1995.

20. The remarks of Foreign Minister Abe, and William Horsley's "No Big Deal Out There," were carried in the August 1985 issue of *No.1 Shimbun*, going to press a month late.

21. "*Tobira hiraketa no wa 'gaiatsu' ka*" ("Was It 'Foreign Pressure' that Opened the Door?"), *Asahi Shinbun*, 3 February 1993.

22. Clayton Jones, "Bloomberg and the Kisha Clubs," *No.1 Shimbun*, October 1992.

23. "Kisha Clubs," *No.1 Shimbun*, July 1993.

24. According to *The Japanese Press: 1995* (published by the Nihon Shinbun Kyokai) there were 181 Japanese correspondents stationed in the U.S. in 1995. The most meaningful comparison would be the 56 Americans stationed in Japan as correspondents for the U.S. media in 1995, according to figures received courtesy of the Foreign Press Center in Tokyo. (This figure does not include American local hires and freelancers, or Japanese and third-country citizens working for American news firms in Japan.)

25. "Managing the Media," *Mainichi Daily News*, 9 December 1992.

26. Carl Johnston, "Japanese Press Short of Space in Washington," *Asian Wall Street Journal*, 10 July 1990. I was interviewed on camera by CNN, Tokyo, on the same subject later that month as some of the American press briefly bit on the bait.

27. Quoted by Robert Whiting, "Prying Open Japan's Press Clubs."

28. Gregory Clark, "Foreign Press Carps at Sources that Feed It," *Nikkei Weekly*, 21 December 1992.

29. Michael Shari, "Financial News Wires Pressing Kisha Clubs for More Access," *Nikkei Weekly*, reprinted in *No.1 Shimbun*, November 1992; Steven Brull, "Japan Press Clubs Open Doors, Slowly," *International Herald Tribune*, 23 July 1993.

30. Quoted in Peter Hadfield, "Political Kingpin Undergoes Pardon Ceremony," *Mainichi Daily News*, 13 June 1993.

31. *Ibid.*

32. Eamonn Fingleton, *Blindside: Why Japan Is Still on Track to Overtake the U.S. by the Year 2000*, New York, Houghton Mifflin, 1995, pp. 266–69.

33. Fumio Kitamura, "Internationalization and Press Clubs," *No.1 Shimbun*, February 1993. Mr. Kitamura was at the time managing director of the Foreign Press Center.

34. Richard Halloran, "Groping through the Chrysanthemum Curtain," *No.1 Shimbun*, December 1968.

35. Quoted by Robert Whiting, "Prying Open Japan's Press Clubs," p. 15.

3 ACADEMIC APARTHEID:
THE PERIPHERAL PROFESSORIATE

1. This survey was conducted by the Wakakusa Law Firm of Nara on behalf of one of the *kyoshi*, John McAteer (under the pen name of John Freeman), whose report on it with comments by fellow *kyoshi* has been circulated privately in Japan. A copy of the Monbusho's telephoned directions, as written down and distributed to Japanese staff at one of the national universities, has been reprinted in Japanese with English translation in *Working Paper No. 3*, Japan Policy Research Institute, Cardiff, Calif., October 1994. It reads in part: " . . . we have been requesting the cooperation of all universities to employ younger people as far as possible . . . we see that you are employing people who . . . are now at pay grades as high as 6 and 7. . . . We want you to tell us how your university plans to deal with such people in the future. . . . With a

limited budget . . . the Ministry will have no alternative but to reduce the number of foreign teachers." My translation.

2. From "Survey Comments" collated by John Freeman. See preceding footnote.

3. For international press coverage of these efforts see letter of Ambassador Mondale to Ivan Hall, "Walter Mondale Addresses Japan's Cartels of the Mind," *JPRI Critique*, Vol. II, No. 6, Japan Policy Research Institute, Cardiff, Calif., June 1995; Dennis Normile, "Japan: Universities Yank Welcome Mat for Longterm Foreign Faculty," *Science*, Vol. 269, 7 July 1995; and Beverly Findlay-Kaneko, "Foreign Teachers Fight to Save Jobs in Japan's National Universities," *The Chronicle of Higher Education*, 28 July 1995.

4. From a copy of the Monbusho reply of 25 April 1995, forwarded to me by the American Embassy. Compare the text of the Monbusho directive given in footnote 1.

5. Telephone conversation with Paul P. Blackburn, Minister-Counselor for Public Affairs, American Embassy, Tokyo, 27 January 1995.

6. For the threat to close down CULCON and the Commission's being "blind" to matters in Japan, see the letter of 6 February 1996, to Ivan Hall from Eric J. Gangloff, Executive Director of the Japan-U.S. Friendship Commission, which also serves as secretariat for the American side of CULCON.

7. For the Diet interpellations see: *Sangiin: Dairokubu: Bunkyo Iinkai Kaigiroku* (Upper House: Part VI: Proceedings of the Education Committee), No. 7, 7 May; and No. 9, 21 May 1996. My translation.

8. Letter from David Wright to Richard H. Simpson, 27 February 1996.

9. From the galley proofs for an amendment to be attached to other legislation, 104th Congress, 2nd Session, received from the office of Sen. Bingaman, 19 April 1996.

10. Shigeru Sheena, "Gaikokujin Kyoshi Sabetsu Mondai no Honshitsu" (The Essence of the Problem of Discrimination Against Foreign Instructors), *Ronza*, October 1996.

11. For the number of Japanese universities, students, professors, and fulltime foreign staff see the *Statistical Abstract of Education, Science, Sports and Culture*, Tokyo, Ministry of Education, Science, Sports and Culture [the Monbusho], 1996, pp. 73–86. The breakdown for foreign professors and associate professors is from *Gakko Kihon Chosa Hokokusho: Koto Kyoiku Hen* (Report on the Basic Survey of Schools: Higher Education), Tokyo, Monbusho, 1995, p. 150. Figures for foreign *kyoshi* and *kyoin* are from unpublished inhouse tables received courtesy of the Monbusho. The figure of 1,312 foreigners at national universities given in the *Statistical Abstract* includes over 400 young *joshu*, or professorial assistants, the lowest staff echelon and concentrated in laboratory sciences, who are hired under their own system. The Ministry of Education, pleading the need for personal privacy and the avoidance of invidiousness, refuses to identify by name, nationality, academic field, or educational background those *kyoin* who do not have fixed-term contracts. The only way to establish a reliable profile of this tenured minority is to locate a personnel officer at each campus who is willing to provide such infor-

mation—a feat last attempted by *Nature* magazine in 1993 (David Swinbanks, "Japanese Universities are Slow to Welcome Foreign Faculty," *Nature*, Vol. 363, 27 May 1993, p. 290).

12. The full title of the new law is: "Kokuritsu mata wa Koritsu Daigaku ni okeru Gaikokujin Kyoin no Ninyo ni kansuru Tokubetsu Shochi Ho"—the "Special Measures Act for the Appointment of Foreign Staff at National or Public Universities."

13. The proposals to place foreigners at private universities, as well as Japanese at all universities, on a contract system were carried in interim form in "Dai Yon-ki Daigaku Shingikai Toshin/Hokoku-Shu" (Fourth Advisory Report/Collected Reports of the University Advisory Council), November 1995, pp. 9–10, 69–72. The final recommendations were issued on 29 October 1996, and widely commented on in the press, but they will not be available in published form until 1997.

14. Based on personal interviews and in-house materials received from foreign and Japanese staff at Waseda and Keio Universities in 1994.

15. Kazuyuki Kitamura, *Daigaku Kyoiku no Kokusaika* (The Internationalization of University Education), Tokyo, Tamagawa Daigaku Shuppanbu, 1984, pp. 68–74.

16. Statistics and listing practice as conveyed by the International Institute of Education, New York, in a telephone conversation on 23 April 1996.

17. The Japan Foundation, *Directory of Japan Specialists and Japanese Studies Institutions in the United States and Canada*, Vol. 1 ("Japan Specialists"), Tokyo, 1995.

18. *Guide to Japanese Studies, 1993–1995*, Center for Japanese Studies, University of Hawaii at Manoa; and *The George Washington University Bulletin: Undergraduate Programs 1995–1996*, Washington, D.C.

19. *Princeton Alumni Weekly*, 7 April 1993.

20. My translation from Tetsujiro Inoue, *Kaikyuroku* (Reminiscences), 1943, as quoted in Kitamura, *Daigaku Kyoiku no Kokusaika*, p. 40. I am indebted to Professor Kitamura, both personally and through his book, for most of the technical and historical discussion of the foreign tenure question in this chapter.

21. See tables for 1886–1934, *ibid.*, pp. 46–47.

22. OECD, *Reviews of National Policies for Education—Japan*, Paris, 1971, pp. 109–112.

23. Quoted in the *Asahi Shinbun*, 19 July 1980, p. 3; my translation. This "self-evident legal principle" (*tozen no hori*), a bureaucratic ruling without any basis in Diet legislation, was invoked once again in 1996 to prevent prefectural and city governments from employing foreigners (mainly the resident Koreans) in supervisory positions at publicly-run institutions such as hospitals and local government offices.

24. Kitamura, *Daigaku Kyoiku no Kokusaika*, pp. 83–84.

25. Except for an occasional explanatory aside, I have based my account of Professor Kang's struggle and the situation of the other three dismissed *kyoshi* entirely on the published record as follows: verbatim text of interviews in the

Tsukuba Gakusei Shinbun (Tsukuba Student Newspaper), 10 June 1985; Margarete Sawada, "Taiho shita Kokusaisei: Tsukuba Daigaku no Baai" (Internationalism in Retreat: The Case of Tsukuba University), *Chuo Koron*, August 1985; Dong Jin Kang, "Damasare Suterareta Gaikokujin Kyoshi" (Deceived and Cast Away Foreign Instructors) and Toshio Usui, "'Don' Fukuda Nobuyuki Gakucho no Sensei Shihai" (The Autocratic Rule of 'Don' President Nobuyuki Fukuda), *Asahi Jaanaru*, 27 September 1985; and the *Asahi Shinbun* for 6 and 9 October 1985. All translations are my own. For English-language reportage see the issues of *Nature* for 10 October 1985 (Vol. 317, pp. 463–65) and 21 November 1985 (Vol. 18, p. 203), and letters to the editor in the *Daily Yomiuri* of 30 March and the *Asahi Evening News* of 10 and 24 May 1985.

26. Sawada, "Taiho shita Kokusaisei," p. 106.

27. *Ibid.*, p. 106.

28. Alun Anderson, "Tsukuba University: Turmoil Over Treatment of Foreign Staff," *Nature*, Vol. 317, 10 October 1985, p. 465. See also the editorial, "Fair Play for Foreigners," p. 463.

29. Ivan Hall, "Nihon no Koto Kyoiku no 'Kokusaika' ni tsuite," ("On the 'Internationalization' of Japan's Higher Education"), *Gendai no Koto Kyoiku* (Modern Higher Education), No. 272, May–June 1986. A year later I introduced the incident in the *Wall Street Journal* ("Stop Making Excuses for Japan's Insularity," 6 July 1987).

30. For the quotations see Kitamura, *Daigaku Kyoiku no Kokusaika*, pp. iv–vii. My translation.

31. My paraphrase and the quotation are from the entry for 22 November 1901, in the diary of Erwin Baelz, Toku Baelz, ed., *Awakening Japan: the Diary of a German Doctor*, Bloomington, Indiana University Press, 1974, p. 151; translated from the German, *Das Leben eines deutschen Arztes im erwachenden Japan*, Stuttgart, J. Engelhorns Nachfolger, 1931.

4 PASSING PRESENCES: SCIENTIFIC RESEARCHERS AND FOREIGN STUDENTS

1. Daniel I. Okimoto, *Between MITI and the Market: Japanese Industrial Policy for High Technology*, Stanford, Stanford University Press, 1989, p. 68.

2. National Science Foundation, *Foreign Participation in U.S. Academic Science and Engineering: 1991*, NSF 93-302, Washington, D.C., 1993.

3. Institute of International Education, *Open Doors 1994/1995: Report on International Educational Exchange*, New York, 1995, pp. 26, 183. See the discussion referenced by footnote 16 in Chapter 3 for the visa status of foreign scholars and researchers covered by IIE statistics.

4. National Science Foundation, *Foreign Participation*, p. 85.

5. Personal communication from the NIH, February 1996.

6. A survey covering JFY 1992 from NEDO (New Energy and Industrial Technology Development Organization), Tokyo, 1994. Courtesy of the NSF Tokyo Office, American Embassy.

7. Donald H. Dalton and Manuel G. Serapio, Jr., *U.S. Research Facilities of Foreign Companies*, U.S. Department of Commerce, Japan Technology Program, Washington, D.C., 1993.

8. Stephanie Epstein, *Buying the American Mind: Japan's Quest for U.S. Ideas in Science, Economics Policy and the Schools*, Washington, D.C., The Center for Public Integrity, 1991, pp. 52–53.

9. Glyn O. Phillips, *Innovation and Technology Transfer in Japan and Europe: Industry-Academic Interactions*, London, Routledge, 1989, Chap. 2.

10. Okimoto, *Between MITI and the Market*, p. 69.

11. I have drawn here in part on presentations by Mary C. Brinton, John W. Dower, Leslie Helm, Richard J. Samuels, and Frank Upham at a workshop on "Intellectual Access in Japan," organized by the Massachusetts Institute of Technology and funded by the Japan-U.S. Friendship Commission, that I attended as a presenter in May 1994. Some of this unpublished material proved useful to the American side of the January 1995 CULCON meeting in Tokyo, which secured Japanese agreement to work for improved access to Japanese data-bases.

12. *Japan Times*, 13 April 1988.

13. British Chamber of Commerce in Japan, Science and Technology Action Group, *Gaijin Scientist: How to Find a Research Post in Japan and What It's Like When You Get There*, Tokyo, 1990.

14. See for example *ibid.*, or Japan Techno-Economics Society, "The Work Environments and Contributions of Foreign Scientists in Japan," Tokyo, May 1994.

15. National Science Foundation, *The United States-Japan Cooperative Science Program: The Thirty Year Report 1961–1990*, Division of International Programs, Washington D.C., 1992.

16. The program statistics are from the National Science Foundation, Tokyo Office, "Current Status of Programs to Support American Researchers in Japan," Report Memorandum No. 94-7, November 1994. Based on U.S. FY1994 and on April 1993–March 1994 for Japanese fiscal year accounting, they incorporate a small percentage, unspecified in the report, for the American humanists and social scientists who participate in JSPS and Fulbright programs. To that extent, the totals given here overstate the actual participation of American scientists and engineers.

17. National Science Foundation, Tokyo Office, "Japanese Companies Hosting American Researchers," Report Memorandum No. 95-21, November 1995.

18. National Science Foundation, Tokyo Office, *Directory of Japanese Company Laboratories Willing to Receive American Researchers*, March 1991.

19. British Chamber of Commerce in Japan, *Gaijin Scientist*, pp. 25, 64–66.

20. Mark Z. Taylor, "Dominance Through Technology: Is Japan Creating a Yen Bloc in Southeast Asia?" *Foreign Affairs*, Vol. 74, No. 6, November/December 1995.

21. National Science Foundation, *Asia's New High-Tech Competitors*, NSF

95-309, Arlington, Va., 1995.

22. The statistics on *ryugakusei* in this chapter are from "Foreign Students in Japan: An Update," Report Memorandum No. 96-8, U.S. National Science Foundation Tokyo Office, 13 March 1996 (for 1995), which updates some of the data in the *Statistical Abstract of Education, Science and Culture*, Ministry of Education, Science and Culture, Tokyo, 1996 (for 1995). As of 1995 the respective percentages for fields of study were 31.3 in the social sciences; 19.6 in the humanities; 19.6 in engineering; 11.5 in medical, agricultural, and basic sciences.

23. *Japan Times*, 24 July 1988.

24. Jesse Wong, "Asian Students Learn to Dislike Japan: After Stint at Japanese Universities, Many Return Home Embittered," and "Japanese Acknowledge Prejudice Lingers," *Asian Wall Street Journal*, 13 February 1996.

25. See for example Roger Goodman, *Japan's 'International Youth': The Emergence of a New Class of Schoolchildren*, Oxford, Clarendon Press, 1990. The *kikokushijo* whom Goodman studied were those being processed through special secondary-level "reception schools" (*ukeireko*) prior to entering Japanese universities. The *kikokushijo* I taught at Tsukuba and Keio, two of the universities drawing the cream of the crop, had nearly all come directly from their secondary schools abroad, and to that extent were even more powerfully acculturated to foreign ways upon arrival as college freshmen.

26. Quote by ambassador Mondale in *Asahi Evening News*, 10 November 1993. Precise figures from National Science Foundation, "Foreign Students in Japan."

27. For a recent survey of this issue see Pat Murdo, "American Students in Japan: Educational Imbalances and Opportunities," JEI Report #8A, Washington, D.C., Japan Economic Institute, 3 March 1995. For the Bridging Project, see *The Commissioner*, Vol. 2, No. 2, Washington, D.C., Japan-U.S. Friendship Commission, Summer–Fall 1995; and "Japan to Lure U.S. Students," *Asahi Evening News*, 7 November 1995.

28. "Toward More Effective U.S.-Japan Exchanges: Challenges and Opportunities," report and recommendations by the Oiso Kenkyukai, December 1994. Available from the United States Information Service, American Embassy, Tokyo.

29. Akimasa Mitsuta, "Surveying Some Differences between American Education and Japanese Education: Why Is It So Difficult for American Students to Study in Japan?" a speech given at the National Association of Foreign Student Advisers (NAFSA) conference on "Breaking Through the Barriers: Alternative Program for U.S. Students in Japan," 2 June 1994.

30. The problems of the branch campuses in both countries were extensively covered by Tokyo's English-language papers during 1990–1994 and reflected the highly negative press given the American branches in Japan by the Japanese media. A more generous evaluation of the new contacts thereby developed was rendered by Gail Chambers and William Cummings in *Profiting from Education: Japan-United States International Educational Ventures in the 1980s*, IIE

Research Report No. 20, New York, Institute of International Education, 1990.

31. I have this anecdote, about his own family, directly from James Fallows, then with *The Atlantic Monthly*.

5 MANIPULATED DIALOGUE:
COWING THE CRITICS

1. *Japan Times*, 22 February 1991.

2. *Asahi Evening News*, 9 March 1991.

3. The term "revisionism" for the new analytical approach to Japan, as well as the "godfather" sobriquet for Chalmers Johnson, were coined by Tokyo bureau chief Robert C. Neff for the 7 August 1989, issue of *Business Week*. Johnson's seminal work, *MITI and the Japanese Miracle*, with its central insight into the "developmental state" had appeared from the Stanford University Press in 1982.

4. New York, Alfred A. Knopf, 1989.

5. Karel van Wolferen, "The Japan Problem," *Foreign Affairs*, Spring 1987.

6. Speech by Glen S. Fukushima at the International House of Japan, Tokyo, 29 October 1985, as published in the *IHJ Bulletin*, Spring 1986.

7. For example, "Stop Making Excuses for Japan's Insularity," *Wall Street Journal*, 6 July 1987; "Kyokuron Medatsu Nihongawa no Shucho" (The Twisted Arguments Conspicuous in Japan's Contention), *Sankei Shinbun*, 20 April 1988; "Nihon no Chishikijin yo, Motto Yuki o!" (To Japanese Intellectuals: Have More Courage!), *Chuo Koron*, August 1989; "America as Japan's Puppet," review of Pat Choate, *Agents of Influence*, *Los Angeles Times*, 28 October 1990; "Memory and Infamy: Why Japan Won't Remember," *Washington Post*, 1 December 1991; "Samurai Legacies, American Illusions," *The National Interest*, No. 28, Summer 1992; "Japan's Asia Card," *The National Interest*, No. 38, Winter 1994/95; "Nihon no Kokuritsu Daigaku ni okeru Apartoheito" (Apartheid at Japan's National Universities), *Ronza*, Vol. 1, No. 2, May 1995.

8. Akira Sono, "Gaiatsu o Yobikomu 'Yuiga Konjo'" (The Egoistic Spirit that Calls in Foreign Pressure), *Sankei Shinbun*, 8 May 1988, referring to my own *Sankei* op-ed column as listed in the preceding footnote. My translation.

9. Tokyo, Ministry of Education, 1937.

10. In the introductory section of an in-house study by the Chosa Kenkyushitsu (Survey and Research Office) of the *Asahi Shinbun*, April 1987. For fuller coverage of the agenda encompassed by *kokusaika* see Hiroshi Mannari and Harumi Befu, eds., *The Challenge of Japan's Internationalization: Organization and Culture*, Kyoto, Kwansei Gakuin and Kodansha International Ltd., 1983.

11. Far-fetched and entertaining examples of uniqueness theory could be cited at length, but there is at hand a fine scholarly study of the subject by Peter N. Dale, *The Myth of Japanese Uniqueness*, Oxford, Nissan Institute and Croom Helm Ltd., 1986; reprinted by Routledge, London, 1988. To note here only a few of the most influential writings (all but the final entry by well-

known academics), two of the earliest works were serious scholarly attempts to apply new frameworks of analysis to Japanese social structure and interpersonal psychology, and essentially nonideological in their original intent:

(a) Chie Nakane, *Tate Shakai no Ningen Kankei: Tanitsu Shakai no Riron* (Personal Relations in a Vertical Society: A Theory of Homogeneous Society), Tokyo, Kodansha, 1967; translated as *Japanese Society*, Berkeley, University of California Press, 1970.

(b) Takeo Doi, *Amae no Kozo* (The Structure of Amae), Tokyo, Kobundo, 1971; translated as *The Anatomy of Dependence*, Tokyo, Kodansha International, 1973.

Most *nihonjinron* writing, however, conveys politically consequential messages concerning the self-contained and impenetrable nature of Japanese culture—a regression to the fundamental prewar cultural assumption of *Kokutai no Hongi*. The most prolific line emphasizes the inner world of consciousness, language, and brain function:

(c) Yuji Aida, *Nihonjin no Ishiki Kozo* (The Structure of Japanese Consciousness), Tokyo, Kodansha, 1970.

(d) Shoichi Watanabe, *Nihongo no Kokoro* (The Heart [Mind, Spirit] of the Japanese Language), Tokyo, Kodansha, 1974.

(e) Tadanobu Tsunoda, *Nihonjin no No: No no Hataraki to Tozai no Bunka* (The Brain of the Japanese: Brain Function and the Cultures of East and West), Tokyo, Taishukan Shoten, 1978.

Most influential in suggesting the essential irrelevance of Western political and social nostrums to Japan's self-generated line of national development was:

(f) Shumpei Kumon, Yasusuke Murakami and Seizaburo Sato, *Bunmei toshite no Ie Shakai* (The Ie [traditional Japanese household] Society as a Civilization), Tokyo, Chuo Koronsha, 1979.

Finally, the wave of popular obsession with Japanese identity as delineated through contrasts to other peoples was set off by a slapdash best seller of the "national character" school:

(g) Isaiah Ben-Dasan (pen name for Shichibei Yamamoto), *Nihonjin to Yudaiyajin*, Tokyo, Yamamoto Shoten; translated as *The Japanese and the Jews*, New York and Tokyo, Weatherhill, 1972.

12. Stan Sesser, "Hidden Death," *The New Yorker*, 14 November 1994.

Acknowledgments

Without unstinting encouragement and assistance from three very special friends, this book would have died on the computer or on some publisher's doorstep. Professor Chalmers Johnson and Mr. James Fallows not only sustained my faith in the topic and in my own writing but also took precious time to read the manuscript in its entirety and to help me find an American publisher while residing in Japan. The United States is lucky to have a noted Asia scholar and a ranking Washington journalist who do not fear to report Japan as they see it, and encourage others to do likewise. I am also deeply indebted to Dr. Sheila Johnson for her infectious good cheer and for her masterful stylistic editing of my entire text.

For the inception of this volume I must thank Dr. Daniel J. Boorstin, who first suggested to me a decade ago the merits of discussing Japanese insularism across a broad spectrum of intellectual institutions. For its completion I am much obliged to Mr. Edwin Barber, my genial editor at W. W. Norton, who inspired a very sensible last-minute reshaping.

My warm gratitude goes to Mr. Eamonn Fingleton, Mr. Robert F. Grondine, and Professors Akio and Margarete Sawada for having read and commented on individual chapters. For valuable insights and materials on Japanese law, higher education, and scientific exchanges I am under obligation, respectively, to Mr. Shigeru Sheena, Professor Kazuyuki Kitamura, and Dr. Larry H. Weber. For his public backing and definitive legal opinion in a personal case related to issues in this book, I am forever grateful to Professor Hisashi Miyajima, one of Japan's leading authorities on labor law. For moral support or help along the way I also want to express my appreciation to Mr. Eliot Hawkins, Mr. Warren Iwasa, Mr. R. Taggart Murphy, Father James B. Simpson, Mr. Karel van Wolferen, the ever-diligent library staff of the Foreign Correspondents' Club of Japan, and certain journalist friends who prefer to remain anonymous. For any deficiencies of fact, expression, or judgment in these pages I, of course, assume the sole responsibility.

I wish to acknowledge the adaptation in my third and fifth chapters of a few paragraphs that have appeared elsewhere: from my article, "Samurai Legacies, American Illusions," in *The National Interest*, No. 28, Summer 1992; and from my chapter contribution, "Creativity Without Diversity? The Anomalous Case of the Japanese University," submitted in 1993 to the Luxembourg Institute for European and International Studies for their conference volume on *The Vitality of Japan: Sources of National Strength and Weakness*, edited by Armand Clesse, Takashi Inoguchi, E. B. Keehn, and J. A. A. Stockwin, to be published in 1997 by Macmillan London Ltd.

To Father William and Mrs. Ann Hargett for repeated stay-overs at St. Alban's Rectory, Tokyo; to my weekend neighbors, Mr. Hunter and Mrs. Eiko Brumfield, for hearty meals and conversation; and to Mr. Kintaro Watanabe and the friendly shopkeepers of Misaki seaport: thanks to all of you for buoying up my spirits during two years' rustication on a windswept bluff overlooking the Pacific.

This book is dedicated with love to my sister Mara Hall Sahl and to my nephew Benjamin Sahl, who with the sharp eye and sound ear of a professional playwright read some of my earlier drafts.

Misaki, Japan
April 1997

Index

keiretsu (business cartels), 77, 130
kenji (public prosecutors), 21
Khrushchev, Nikita, 154
kikokushijo (repatriated children), 143
Kim Dae Jung, 65-66
Kirk, Donald, 63
kisha kaiken (on-the-record press conferences), 52, 55, 57, 59, 61-62, 66-69, 70, 71, 75, 182
kisha kurabu (journalists' clubs), 45-48, 50, 52-79
Kitamura, Kazuyuki, 121
"kitchen debate" (1959), 154
Kobayashi, Hisashi, 100
Kobe earthquake, 77, 178
kokka komuin (state officials), 87
kokumin kanjo (national sentiment), 151
kokusaika (internationalization), 7, 19-20, 25, 83, 85, 88, 94, 101, 107, 113-14, 117, 121, 124, 133-34, 143, 147-48, 149, 156-58, 161, 172-79, 182-83
Kokutai no Hongi (Fundamental Principles of the National Polity), 173
kondan (off-the-record background briefings), 52, 54, 57, 59, 62, 67-68, 69, 75
Kosaka, Masataka, 165
Kusakabe, Kiyoko, 84-85
Kyocera, 128
kyodo jigyo (joint enterprises), 28-29, 33-34, 44
kyoin (teaching staffers), 92-96, 103-10, 112, 118, 119
Kyoin Law (1982), 94-95, 103, 104
kyoshi system, 80-89, 92-96, 102-3, 107, 109, 110, 113-14, 116, 118-19, 121
Kyoto University, 105

laboratories, 8, 123, 124, 129-30, 136
Labor Standards Act (Rodo Kijun Ho), 87, 97
law:
  on academics, 86-87
  contract, 43
  human rights and, 30-31, 34, 35
  international, 23-24, 27, 28-29, 30, 33, 36
  on lawyers, 24, 30, 35
  press, 51, 53
  U.S., 22-23, 30, 31-32
lawsuits, 30, 34-35, 87, 97, 170
lawyers, 17-44
  academics compared with, 88-89

  barriers against, 7, 8, 17-44, 182
  competition of, 18, 24-25, 30, 31-34
  corporate, 18, 20, 23, 24, 26, 27, 32, 33, 34, 35, 38-39, 40
  "cultural differences" of, 24, 29-37
  education of, 20-22, 26-27, 37-39
  as elite, 20-22, 35
  ethical standards for, 29-31, 34, 35
  European, 43-44
  firms for, 23, 24-27, 29, 31, 32, 38
  foreign-trained, 26-27
  gaiben designation for, 27-29, 32-33, 34, 38, 40, 43
  "guild" for, 20
  isolation of, 35-36, 182
  in Japan vs. U.S., 21, 22-26, 29-32, 36-37, 120
  joint enterprises for, 28-29, 33-34, 44
  journalists compared with, 46, 48, 72
  litigation, 20-26, 29, 31, 33, 35, 36, 38, 39, 40, 42
  long-term positions for, 24-25
  market for, 31-32, 33, 37, 42-43
  numerical restrictions on, 20, 22, 34, 37
  organizations of, 25, 28, 89
  qualifications of, 21, 22, 26, 30, 37-39
  reforms for, 24, 25-29, 32, 40, 41-44
  regulation of, 24-25, 30, 35
  residency requirements for, 38
  salaries for, 30, 33
  status of, 24-25, 27-29, 31, 35-36
  technical standards for, 30, 37-40
Lawyers Law (Bengoshi Ho) (1949), 24, 30, 35
"legal advisors," 21-22
"legal consultants," 24
Legal Research and Training Institute (LRTI), 20-22, 26, 30, 37
Leipzig, University of, 86
Liberal Democratic Party (LDP), 65, 67
Library of Congress, U.S., 131
Lugar, Richard, 145

MacArthur, Douglas, 55
Mansfield, Mike, 13, 185
Manufacturing Technology Fellowships, 135
markets, 33, 45-46, 76
  academic, 119
  closed, 8-9, 17, 42, 175
  intellectual, 18
  legal, 31-32, 33, 37, 42-43
  open, 8, 11, 83, 124, 164, 175, 178, 180
Marshall Fund, 162
Massachusetts Institute of Technology (MIT), 100, 128